Space to Breathe, Room to Grow

Jill Briscoe
Judy Briscoe Golz

For Her. For God. For Real.
faithfulwoman.com

Faithful Woman is an imprint of
Cook Communications Ministries, Colorado Springs, Colorado 80918
Cook Communications, Paris, Ontario
Kingsway Communications, Eastbourne, England

SPACE TO BREATHE, ROOM TO GROW
© 2002 by Jill Briscoe and Judy Golz. All rights reserved.

First printing, 1985
First revised printing, 2002
Printed in the United States of America.
1 2 3 4 5 6 7 8 9 10 Printing/Year 05 04 03 02

Senior Editor: Janet Lee
Cover Design: Image Studios
Cover Photography: Photodisc, Inc.
Interior Design: Image Studios

Library of Congress Cataloging-in-Publication Data

CIP data application filed

To Greg and Stuart,
the special men in our lives
who have lovingly given us
space to breathe
and
room to grow
in every dimension,
not least in the area
of our own precious
mother-daughter relationship.

Judy and Jill

Judy Briscoe Cox

Jill Briscoe

A Prayer

Oh Spirit of love
Christ my Savior
Come to my heart.

I would be born from above
to belong to Your
family.

May the people I care most about see the difference.

Lord, enroll me in school,
the school of
Your
world.

To learn the lessons of love.

Amen.

Contents

Love is a Choice

CHAPTER ONE

Does "belonging" belong to us? Do we have the inalienable right to be private? Can two people struggle to relate in the twilight zone? Two "Christian" people? Can the test tube relationships of believers develop normally in the laboratory of such sterile scrutiny?

As a new Christian, I was introduced as a matter of course to the public's "right to know"—the right to know everything about my relationships, for example. My relationships with God, fellow believers, and even unbelieving friends I had recently counted so dear were now under public scrutiny. Too many times, public prayer meetings publicized private confidences. My early struggles were tenderly targeted for caring—and sharing—with total strangers in that supposedly "close" circle of bent heads.

English by nationality, I had been raised with the conviction that the Englishman's home was his castle, and his relationships were the most personal and private of his possessions. They were to be his business and his alone. The moat of cool aloofness would quite rightly isolate any outsider who might rudely intrude and want to know "too much."

The initial shock of the discovery that my new friends were quietly but incessantly relating the progress of my Christian growth to whoever wanted to hear about it nearly capsized my early faith. Fresh faith withers when it discovers it can't trust the faithful to keep faith—or in plainer terms, to keep their mouths shut!

But as people around me continued to talk "honestly" about their own struggles, and particularly their people differences, I learned a valuable lesson. I found myself relieved of the unrealistic expectations I had placed upon myself concerning my relationships within this strange new circle of constant company. After all, before I became a Christian, I had freely chosen my own friends. Now I was informed that Christ had chosen them for me! What a relief it was to learn other believers found this as hard as I did. I will never forget a rather unpleasant lady barreling up to me after a meeting and saying, "The Lord has told me to be your friend—your close friend," she added firmly in case I had misunderstood!

"Lord," I said under my breath, "why did You tell her that? Surely You know I would never choose such a person for a friend!"

As it turned out, I needn't have worried about it because she suddenly lost her job and was transferred to the other end of the country. This led me to wonder if perhaps the Lord had not told her any such thing! Hearing someone else relate a similar incident helped me to deal with the guilt arising from my reaction.

It wasn't easy working it all out. In fact, it was very difficult indeed. We all need help in this regard, as life itself is made up of relationships. This is where we live our lives, shed our tears, and are driven to despair or carried to ecstasy. To relate is to belong, and to belong is to know we are loved and needed and are therefore of immense value.

The tactful, careful openness of a few mature people in the months following my conversion convinced me of the necessity of sharing selected relational experiences for the encouragement of the family of God. If I had been relieved by such disclosures, then it behooved me to return the compliment.

As my ministry expanded, I found people identified with an honest recounting of my fears and failures as well as my triumphs. When I would talk about losing my temper as a young mother struggling to establish friendship at such an infant level, faces would light up in the audience. "I know about that," the faces would say, "I've been there!" Now the woman on the platform was not some clever, complete guide to perfection, but rather a sympathetic fellow traveler along the same rough road. She was sharing the secrets of "belonging" learned at no small cost, building a bridge across a sea of strangers, enabling them to meet and mull over some aspect of truth that would help them both to grapple with whatever relational problem happened to be under discussion.

The conviction that such sharing can be of help to others is the rationale for this book. Judy and I will seek to share a relationship that could be considered one of our most private and precious possessions—our mother/daughter link of love. Judy, our only daughter, is the middle child of three; born to belong to the Briscoes for twenty-one years and now to Greg till "death do them part." Judy's marriage has not severed our relationship—only the dependence upon a mother who has come to appreciate her daughter on a grand new level. Judy's new status has, in fact, enabled us all to start learning the lessons of love all over again.

Some time ago, as we began to share a ministry together, Judy and I found the most meaningful and helpful material we could teach had to do with relationships and, specifically, with the examples we gleaned together from the fertile fields of the book of Ruth. Planted in the Old Testament, this truly historical account gives us, among other things, examples of many and varied relationships that lend themselves well to personal application. We discovered we could identify with the human dilemmas and choices that flowed through the narrative.

The story of Ruth and Naomi gave us footholds on a mountain of truth that we climbed together as we talked through our discovery of each other. We turned our findings into usefulness by sharing the lessons that we learned with the Christian community and responding to a suggestion to make our material more permanent by way of the pen. Judy agreed to the writing assignment, though not initially without a little apprehension.

"Do you think I can do it, Mom?" she inquired.

I knew she was not asking me could she do it, rather could she do it well enough. My overachieving daughter was, as usual, questioning her ability to do the "excellent" thing. Her expected response made me not a little ashamed of my readiness to settle for mediocrity! How could one with so much undoubted ability be so unsure of herself, I wondered? What had I done—or left undone—that had caused her to have such a huge lack of confidence? How could one who had lived her life in the constant shape of an "A," be so concerned that she might suddenly produce a "B"? Perhaps we could discover the reason why through the communication this project would involve.

"Why don't you tell the readers a little about yourself, Judy," I suggested. "If people have been able to identify with me when I've shared my fears, it follows they'll be able to relate to you when you share yours. After all," I reminded her, "you know people have really been helped when you've talked about some of your struggles."

Tackling the challenge head-on, in typical fashion, she said, "OK."

I'll tell them how frightened I was when you and I first began to lead meetings together. I was scared that I'd stammer while speaking; scared that people would think I had received the opportunity to speak only because I was Jill Briscoe's daughter; scared that my material was boring and dull; basically, just scared of failing. You know, I've always been petrified of failing.

I knew that this speaking ministry would be difficult because I would have to overcome so many people's expectations of me. But I think the hardest part was that I wanted so desperately to match up to your expectations of me and I didn't know if I could. As usual, I wanted you to be proud of me, yet this was something I couldn't control. Of course, I could prepare adequately, and I did. Yet, as you know, there is more to speaking than just preparing.

Do you remember when we were speaking at our first convention in Australia? We were at Stanwell Tops, the convention site where two thousand women had gathered to listen to Jill Briscoe. I had been given the Saturday evening session to talk about, of all things, handling anxiety! All day long, as I walked around the beautiful site, women told me what a wonderful mother I had, what a phenomenal speaker she was, and how much she had helped them in their spiritual growth. I agreed with everything they said. You know, I'm one of your biggest fans, but those compliments made me feel even more inadequate! Most of the women at the convention were older than I. Why would they be interested in listening to a twenty-two year old? By dinnertime, I had talked myself into a tizzy. I really didn't know if I could even get up on the platform. Finally, I did what I should have done in the beginning. I turned to the Lord. I went to my room and opened my Bible, and guess what I found?

> Praise be to the God and Father of our Lord Jesus Christ, the Father of compassion and the God of all comfort, who comforts us in all our troubles, so that we can comfort those in any trouble with the comfort we ourselves have received from God (2 Corinthians 1:3–4).

"Judy," Jesus said, "I don't know why you are so worried about everyone else's expectations for you. It is only My expectations that really matter. You're right, you won't ever be a Jill Briscoe, but if you let Me, I'll make you My Judy Golz. You have so much to say to these women, not because you have prepared properly, but because I've given you the subject, information, and experience. Remember all those times you were uptight and anxious? Remember how we worked through each situation? Well, go and tell these women how they, too, can find comfort in Me!"

You know, Mom, that was a hard lesson for me to learn. I had become so wrapped up in the performance aspect of public speaking that I lost sight of my real purpose—to minister. I know I can't speak without Jesus enabling me to do so, but with His help, the results are limitless!

I suppose I feel the same way about this book. I'm not a writer, whereas you have written so many books. During the past few weeks, those old feelings of inadequacy have been creeping back into my thoughts. Yet I remember my lesson in Australia.

Judy, writing will give us an opportunity to speak to people we've never met. A book can go to places we will never go. It can be given to a friend in need, a mother struggling with her teenager, or a teenager struggling with her mother. Just think of the possibilities!

OK, I'm convinced. Let's go.

Why don't we start by defining a relationship?

But where will we go from there?

I knew we were going to have trouble doing this together! I like to just "talk" on paper, and I bet you want a neat outline before we even begin.

Well, let's build a bridge across this chasm right from the start. Let's compromise, Mom, and do it my way!

There you go, Judy! So let's define a relationship!

The dictionary says, a relationship is two objects that are in relation to each other. That's a bit obvious, isn't it? This is better—"a sense of belonging"—

I like that!

What about "personal magnetism—a binding together"?

I don't know about the magnetism bit. That makes it sound easy, almost automatic, and I think the majority of relationships are hard work! Magnetism sounds inanimate, but I guess that's OK if you're talking about material objects in relation to one another.

As stars to skies
and sight to eyes,
As leaf to tree
and hive to bee,
As babbling brook
to grassy nook—

That's good, Mom. I like your poetry.

Now you've broken my train of thought—train—hmmmmm …

As stars to sky in close relation
so train is to a railway station.
As leaf to tree and note to song
so things to other things belong.
Inanimate without affections
nature makes its own connections.
But human beings have a choice, to choose to
love—to raise their voice and say,
"I really want to know
 the way you think
before you go and live
your life in other spheres.
Let's share some laughter and some tears—
see—
here's my heart, I'll let you in,
'twill be enlarged when you have been
a part of all its eagerness
to give another … happiness"!

I think that's excellent, Mom. Only living beings can choose to have relationships. A cabbage doesn't have much option about which cabbage it sits next to in its patch, yet animals and humans are different. A dog can choose whether or not to obey its master's call.

Like our dog, you mean?

Not exactly! Every day of Prince's doggy life he chose not to obey any of our calls! But obviously there is something very special about an animal-to-human relationship.

I read about a dog named Barry who saved more than forty people buried in avalanches in the Swiss Alps. He actually dug through as much as twenty feet of snow to rescue them.[1]

That's a good illustration, even though it makes me a bit uncomfortable. I can't help feeling animals do better than humans sometimes! That is, unless you're talking about our dog. I'm sure glad I never had to depend on Prince to find me in an avalanche. He was far too fond of himself to stay outside in a snowstorm for more than five minutes!

Well, if animals have a choice, humans certainly do! There are some great stories about people who needed each other to achieve a common goal. For example, there's Helen Keller and Anne Sullivan Macy's relationship that spanned nearly half a century. They say the blind and deaf girl wasn't the easiest person to teach at first, but Anne chose to stick with the relationship. In fact, she became so indispensable that Helen said, "The most important day I remember in all my life was the one on which my teacher, Anne Mansfield Sullivan, came to me."[2]

And yet, in a sense, you don't choose your helper if you're blind. Such relationships are born out of mutual necessity. I think the hardest thing of all is to choose to have a relationship with a really difficult person you don't even like, much less love, for no other reason than you decide to have it.

Only a Christian would do that.

Exactly. Didn't Jesus say, "'If you love those who love you, what credit is that to you? Even sinners love those who love them'"(Luke 6:32).

I know I wouldn't have bothered working at some of the hard relationships in my life if I hadn't been a Christian.

Me neither. I remember what a mess most of my friendships were in when I first came to Christ. It was a huge shock to my system to realize that when I got right with God, He expected me to get right with everyone else! I can remember being stunned when I discovered the verse that said, "'A new commandment I give to you, that you Love one another; as I have loved you …'" (John 13:34, NKJV). If love is a command, it can be obeyed. That said all sorts of things to me. It told me love is much more than a nice feeling; it involves loving actions, and it showed me I had many decisions to make.

You're right! The majority of our relationships constitute a choice—the choice to love.

A lot depends on our understanding of that word **love**, don't you think?

Sure. If you define love as "a feeling too big for words," then decisions and choices have nothing to do with it. You can't choose to have a feeling.

But you can choose to act lovingly. If God's sort of love is agape love, which means "a primary concern for the other's well-being irrespective of the cost to oneself," then you're in business.

Jesus demonstrated God's love by coming willingly to earth, knowing before He came that He would be crucified for His trouble. I'm quite sure

He didn't feel like being crucified. He was able to think about us and our sinful state and what the awful consequences of that would be if He didn't do something about it. He acted out of His great concern for us.

Anyone can choose to be concerned and do something about it before the feelings ever come along. After all, emotions are a valid but somewhat fickle part of love. Feelings come and feelings go, don't they?

Yes, they do. Think about Ruth and Naomi. There's a great example for you. They chose to be concerned about each other when it must have been very hard to rely on the feeling part of love to carry them through.

Give us the background of the story, Judy.

The scene is set during the time of Judges, a period of Israel's history that was full of rebellion and immorality. At that time, there was a famine in Bethlehem. This was ironic because the name Bethlehem *means "House of Bread."*

Throughout the Scriptures natural disasters were permitted by God as a means of chastening His rebellious people.

Well, whatever the reason, there was no food in Bethlehem, so Elimelech and his wife, Naomi, and their two sons, Mahlon and Chilion, moved to Moab. They knew the Moabites were enemies of God; but because they were desperate to make a living they settled there anyway.
After a while Elimelech died, and the boys married Moabite women. One married Orpah and the other, Ruth. Everyone lived happily for ten years, but then the boys died. Soon afterward, the famine in Bethlehem ended, and Naomi decided to go home. She and her daughters-in-law packed up and started out on the road to Bethlehem. Partway through the journey, they arrived at a crossroad. Naomi turned to her two daughters-in-law and suggested they return to Moab. She wanted the

women to have a security that she couldn't promise them: "Then they lifted up their voices and wept again; and Orpah kissed her mother-in-law, but Ruth clung to her" (Ruth 1:14, NJKV).

There at the crossroad, everyone had a chance to make a choice.

You're right. Orpah, whose name means "stubbornness," apparently decided to kiss her mother-in law good-bye and go her own way. She chose not to have a relationship with Naomi, whereas Ruth, whose name means "Friendship," decided to stick with her. She clung to her mother-in-law.

In other words, she made up her mind she was going to stay with Naomi through all the trials that were ahead. I can't help identifying with that. I had a similar choice to make when Grandma came to stay with us. Ever since we'd come to America, I had dutifully written to Grandma every week. One day I said to your dad, "Why don't you write to your mother this time. She'd much rather hear from you than from me." So he sat down and wrote a lovely, long letter, and I took the week off. Then the answer came, and I couldn't believe it. "My darling Stuart," it began, "I can't tell you how thrilled I was to hear from you, and of course, I'd love to come to stay with you for three months." Three months! I decided I would "never" allow your father to write again! You see Grandma and I were a classic example of a mother-in-law and a daughter-in-law struggling with a difficult relationship. I'd been an Orpah for years, kissing my mother-in-law, but stubbornly going my own way. Now I had a choice: I could borrow strength from God and become a Ruth or return like Orpah to the old way of doing things. True friendship won't settle for selfishness. Friendship says, "I'm going to be your friend whether you want me to or not." I gave up my stubbornness and set about letting God work it out between us.

I never knew you and Grandma didn't get along very well.

There was never open warfare. But when Grandma and I came to that crossroad in our lives, we both had to decide which way we were going to go.

Was that when Grandma discovered she had cancer?

Yes. Remember those last ghastly months when she had so many operations and suffered so much?

Of course I remember. She was so brave!

Judy, if I hadn't been prepared to be a Ruth before that happened, I could never have carried out the necessary love tasks that were needed at that time.

Was it easy to be a Ruth, Mom? I mean, how does it work? Do you just get down on your knees and say, "Yesterday I was an Orpah; from this day on I'll be a Ruth"?

No, of course not. It's a daily thing. I wasn't always a Ruth. Many a time I reverted to being a stubborn Orpah. Once, when I knew Grandma did not approve of a certain mode of dress, I deliberately wore the offending garments even though I had a wardrobe full of clothes I could easily have chosen to wear. Now that was quite juvenile and didn't help the atmosphere in our home! To flaunt one's "rights" may prove a point, but it doesn't build friendship. I had to ask myself, "Would it hurt to wear the sort of clothes that Grandma approves of while she visits us?" The answer to that was, of course, it wouldn't hurt and it would certainly save hurting her! If I could stop being stubborn over a bit of cloth, maybe I'd have more going for me when I felt I did have a case I should argue.

I remember Grandma not liking some of my clothes. She changed a lot though during those months she was with us.

That was because cancer struck again, and suddenly more immediate needs demanded everyone's attention. I was glad then that I'd learned not to act out of my feelings but rather according to the law of love. When it really mattered, God enabled me to be a Ruth even when the feelings weren't there! It doesn't happen all in a day you know—

I know what you're going to say. You don't grow an oak tree overnight!

Exactly. And you don't grow a Ruth relationship overnight either. Friendship grows slowly. Deciding to be a friend is a daily decision for the disciple of Jesus Christ. Grandma and I, for example, had a lot going for us. We both enjoyed a relationship with Jesus, who expected us to have a relationship with each other. When two people are believers, they have the most important thing in common—their faith. Faith is the fertile soil—the common ground that the plant of true friendship can thrive in.

Mother, is that the right picture? Your plants hardly ever survive your loving nurturing!

That's true! But I persevere. Those poor plants of mine know I'm absolutely determined to make them grow!

Before you can grow friendship out of the common ground of faith, you have to be determined to do everything in your power to make it happen.

The problem I have is that I don't always want it to happen. You take a risk when you move close to someone you've kept your distance from for a long time. After all, you reason, if I'm not too sure I even like her from a distance, how can I be sure I'll love her up close?

And then there's the sheer energy that growing a close relationship takes out of you. Initiating friendship takes an awful lot of effort. You have to be sure you want that level of involvement. This may sound funny to you, but when Greg applied to graduate school and had to write an essay on his extracurricular activities during college, he mentioned that he had dated the same woman for three years and eventually married her. He was trying to express the amount of time and effort that had been invested in our relationship.

Growing real friendships will cost. It will mean going the extra mile, doing the things that could be considered unnecessary, thinking up ways of enlarging the space around you on a daily basis so someone can step inside the circle of your world and feel welcome there.

When I first found out that my best friend and I were going to Wheaton, I wanted us to be roommates. It seemed the natural thing to do since Kerrie and I had been inseparable for five years. But when we sat down and talked about it, we realized that sticking so close to each other might be unhealthy and exclude others. So when the time came to send in our housing requests, we asked to be on the same floor but not roommates. Even this was hard because I would always want to turn to Kerrie with my joys and sorrows. I had to learn to let others get close to me. I had to take the time and make the emotional effort to establish new friendships. Now I'm really glad that we forced ourselves to go the extra mile.

For me, growing a friendship with you meant deciding to let you interfere with my duties—my schedule, my responsibilities. I decided to be your friend when I was very big and you were very small. I needed to be reminded of that choice constantly. There were so many things to do when you kids were little, and you can't just stop the doing to be a friend. It meant involvement.

What do you mean?

Well, I couldn't just say, "Blow the baking, we'll play dominos for an hour," or "I'll let the kids wear dirty clothes this week. It's much more important to read them stories." What I did was to share the daily doing with you as my friend. Don't you remember baking with me? We did it nearly every day when you were a little girl.

Yes I do. I remember one of those times especially, even though I was only four years old. We were baking and talking about Sunday school. I asked you a very important question. If I invited Jesus to come and live in my heart, would I still have to put away all of my toys? You, of course, said yes. So I went away for a while. Then I came back and asked you the same question again. I figured that if you really wanted me to become a Christian, you'd be easy on me and say that I didn't have to clean up. But you didn't make it simple, did you? You wanted me to realize that making Jesus Christ the Lord of my life would mean sacrifice and maybe even hardship. Although you answered my question with the same steadfast yes, I still wanted Jesus to come into my life. That afternoon we knelt by the couch, and I asked Him into my heart. It was a special day.

Very special, and it was so simple really. Just a question of doing things **with** you instead of **for** you. Of course, it was slower—

And messier—

But fun!

It works both ways, don't you think? I mean, growing our friendship didn't involve much of a choice for me when I was very small, but it was different when I was a teenager. Then it was my turn to make a choice to be your friend! I had to decide to let you interfere with my schedule for a change.

Explain that to me.

Well, for example, there was the question of shopping. I only wanted you to come if you walked a step behind me. I suppose I was at an age when it wasn't "right" to be seen walking down the mall with your mother. That was a phase where being "in" with the crowd meant only being seen with your peers. But that stage didn't last too long, did it? After a while we began to go shopping whenever we could, especially when you were buying! Not only did we walk next to each other, but also we'd be laughing and giggling and having a great time. Because we chose to do things together, we became best friends!

I liked that. My problem was I didn't understand how hard it was for you. I was far too easily hurt. Most decisions to spend time with your mother instead of your friends when you're a teenager have to be a matter of choice rather than feeling. Now I see how special every one of those times was! I needed to stop being so supersensitive and thank you for all the moments you made me forget I was over forty—for slipping your arm through mine—for giggling and sharing and for saying, "I'm glad we're superclose, Mom!" Can you possibly know what that's worth?

How could I, Mom, until I had children of my own?

Love is Jesus, costly, caring, robed in Galilean cloth—
a carpenter by trade.
Carving out eternal people from His world—
for us to love—as He loves us.
Love treats others with respect—
Because love knows that life's made up
of crossroads—
Pausing places on the trail of time—
Where people—lent the dignity of choice
by Love Himself—
Decide to be a friend.

Love helps the chooser do the hardest thing,
In face of winds of adverse circumstance
In bitter loss, or sickness, or distress
He helps a Ruth, Naomi bless.

Love lets a sister go without a cry
For love respects the choice and will not try
To force the company of one who'd much prefer
to meet her own deep needs—
Love says "good-bye" nor heeds her own sad heart
Love bleeds—but blesses anyway!

The choice is ours, to go with love to Bethlehem
or walk away from friendship—fast
Orpah-like—and stubborn to the last!

Talk Time

1. Read chapter one of Ruth together, taking turns reading the verses.

2. Circle who you feel closest to. Discuss with each other why you answered this way.

Spouse	Mom/Dad	Other _____
Brother/Sister	Dog/Cat	Boyfriend/Girlfriend

3. Relationships rooted in God's love have a firm footing. Define God's sort of love. How did He demonstrate it (John 3:16)?

4. Look up the following verses and talk about them. Pick out one of these verses and give it to each other as a gift.

Proverbs 18:24	Ecclesiastes 4:10
John 15:13	Proverbs 17:17
Proverbs 27:9	

5. What do you like best about Ruth and Naomi's relationship? What do you like best about your relationship? What don't you like about Orpah and Naomi's relationship? What don't you like about your relationship?

Love is a Commitment

CHAPTER TWO

Choosing is just the start. When we choose to be a Ruth—to be a friend—the hard work begins. There has to be a wholehearted commitment of energy and time. Each party has to know the other is totally committed to the process of building on the promises that have been made. I think of the marriage commitment. Marriage has a hard time surviving if one party is forever wondering if the other party really meant what they said when the original commitment was made.

That's very important. Unfortunately, our world doesn't think that way. Years ago, when I was telling my coworkers that I was going to Australia for five weeks, one of my friends asked if Greg was going with me. I said, "No, because Mom and I have been invited to speak exclusively to women." My friend couldn't believe it. He said, "Do you mean to tell me that you actually trust your husband for five weeks without you?" I thought he was teasing me. Unfortunately, he was dead serious, so I took the opportunity to tell him that I did trust Greg because we had committed ourselves to each other, before God, forever.

You know, Judy, when Dad gave me this engagement ring, I expected him to say something wonderfully romantic. I think I had read too much poetry because I was waiting for some beautiful "old world" words—rhetoric that smelled like tea roses after rain.

I can't wait! What happened?

Well, we were downtown in Liverpool—in the rush hour—

Oh, no!

Oh, yes! But, then, I didn't see why a few thousand trucks and buses should spoil our romantic moment! We bought the ring in a little shop. That was the easy part because we knew exactly what we wanted. We had agreed to look for a ring with three stones to represent the Lord Jesus in the midst of our relationship. Sitting in the car, your dad placed the ring on my finger, looked deep into my eyes, and said, "Well, Jill, that's that!" Not the most romantic way of promising me a lifetime commitment would you say?

No, those aren't exactly the most poetic words I've heard!

When we arrived back home after purchasing the ring, my mother was on the phone with the local jeweler. Without our knowing about it, she had told the woman we would probably purchase the ring from her. Embarrassed, she pushed the phone into my hand to explain. Flustered, I spluttered, "Oh, Mrs. Cannel, I'm so sorry, maybe next time!" It was then your dad took the phone out of my hand, took me in his arms, and said quietly and seriously, "Jill, there won't be a next time. Don't you remember, I told you that's that!" Suddenly those two little words became the most romantic words I'd ever heard. Dad committed himself to me, "for better or for worse, for richer or for poorer, in sickness or in health, till death us do part." From that sure foundational promise we began to build our relationship.

Don't you think a relationship has to involve an understanding of commitment? How can you ever enjoy another person if you're scared of losing him/her? You'd always have to perform to please. You could never be yourself.

Exactly. I see Ruth and Naomi choosing to have a deep relationship that involved total commitment, a "that's that" promise. Look at the language:

Entreat me not to leave you,
Or to turn back from following after you;
For wherever you go, I will go;
And wherever you lodge, I will lodge;
Your people shall be my people,
And your God, my God.
Where you die, I will die,
And there will I be buried.
The Lord do so to me, and more also, If anything but death parts you and me (Ruth 1:16–17, NKJV).

Ruth promised Naomi, in effect, that their relationship would be "for better or for worse, for richer or for poorer, in sickness or in health, till death us do part."

And that's a mouthful! When two people stand in front of the preacher on their wedding day, they are not thinking for worse, for poorer, in sickness, or about death! And who can blame them? They are thinking for better, for richer, and in health. But if a lifetime commitment has not been made, the marriage will rock when the storms of life come—and they will come! You can't have a world full of sunshine.

When young couples go through the premarital class at church, we try to emphasize that.

Greg and I enjoyed that class—especially the panel of "experts" you brought into one of the sessions.

You mean the married couples we asked to share their experiences?

Yes. They were great! I liked the way you chose them to represent the negative forces in a marriage. For example, the couple who represented "for richer or poorer."

The poverty-stricken medical student and his young wife?

They were so real. And I'm sure all of us identified. It's hard starting out with very few resources.

Especially when you've been used to living at a comfortable level in your parents' home!

Then there was the woman who had cancer. She and her husband shared the stress her illness brought to their relationship and how God had worked in their particular situation to bring them closer together.

That's unusual, too. So often when one partner develops an incurable disease, the marriage breaks up.

But that's just when you need each other the most!

It's at times like those—when the sunshine hides behind the clouds—that you have to be able to depend on each other.

This whole idea of commitment reminds me of one of my favorite missionaries. What do you know about C. T Studd?

Not much.

He was an illustrious Cambridge college athlete, wealthy beyond measure. He grew up on his father's English estate and was destined to live a life of fame and fortune. So it came as a great shock to many when word spread that he had been converted through D. L. Moody. He sold his horses and began to follow Christ. Six years later, he was considered England's greatest cricketer, and with the world at his feet, he shocked the country when he gave it all up to serve God in China! He married Priscilla, gave away his inheritance—more than half a million dollars—and began an incredible ministry. "For five years," he wrote, "we never went outside our doors without a volley of curses from our neighbors,"[1] but they persisted. After all, they had promised each other for better or for worse, for richer or for poorer.

Wasn't he the man who read a sign on a door that said, "Cannibals want missionaries" and went to Africa without his wife?

Yes, Priscilla was suffering from a debilitating heart condition at the time. He was ill, too, and without financial support, but he went anyway. When he returned home three years later, his only furlough in the last eighteen years of his life, he found his wife recovered and running the home office, which she continued to do until her death thirteen years later. Talk about in sickness and in health, till death us do part! A full commitment like that, with no "option out" clause, gives you the freedom to understand the other person as well as you possibly can. A solid commitment to a given relationship means you set about trying to identify with your partner and to see things the way the other sees them.

Priscilla figured out how to do that practically, didn't she? She learned to identify with her husband's calling.

Understanding C. T.'s background and his total commitment to life in general and the Lord in particular must have helped his wife to identify with her husband and stick with an extremely difficult relationship.

That makes sense to me. Even Naomi and Ruth had to learn about each other's roots. Naomi immigrated to a foreign land and therefore had to understand a different culture and learn new customs. But because Moab wasn't a God-fearing place, Naomi must have had to search very hard to find things that she could appreciate about that strange country.

Naomi wasn't the only person trying to identify with another's background.

True—Ruth had to learn about the Israelite culture, too. After Ruth married, she moved into Naomi's home and had to live and work very closely with her. I'm sure this presented plenty of opportunities to learn about her mother-in-law.

I remember discovering some things about one of your boyfriends that helped me to understand him. My first impressions were negative and I couldn't have cared less where he lived, if he was into sports, what sort of car he drove—anything. But I well remember the first time I ever made the huge effort to sit down and ask (through clenched teeth), "What does your friend want to do when he leaves school?" You've no idea what it cost me to force myself to show even that much interest. You replied, "He wants to go into politics, and he'll probably become the president of the United States. Then I'll tell my friends, just my luck—my mother didn't appreciate him!" But you know, Judy, by asking that one question I got a whole new insight into that young man. If I hadn't asked a question I didn't want to ask, I'd never have begun to appreciate him.

Don't you think you were struggling with a new culture though, Mom? We'd just come here from England. Everything was so new, so different. We all had to get used to pavements being called sidewalks, perambulators, baby buggies, the bonnet and boot of our car, the trunk and hood, and biscuits, cookies.

Culture shock had an awful lot to do with it. But in this case people differences were the main problems. I was too quick to judge. Even within the family circle you've got people differences. Look at Dad and me. We're totally incompatible. That's what attracted me to him in the first place! Opposites attract! Then there are you three kids; look at you. You are incompatible because you are opposites too. But isn't that what family is all about? Five totally incompatible people learning how to make allowances for the differences they discover; learning how to love and understand each other within the safe boundaries of a committed relationship.

What about you and me, Mom? We're different as well. Think about the way we both came to faith. We needed to show respect for each other's perspective and accept one another for who we were, not just for what we believed. You didn't hear about Jesus Christ until you were eighteen. So, in a sense, you grew up like Ruth, not knowing that Jesus died for your sins. On the other hand, I grew up in the Christian home you made for me and accepted Him into my heart when I was four. I was like Naomi. Don't you think Naomi and Ruth had a lot of conflicts throughout their relationship about their beliefs? They must have had to build their share of bridges over some pretty deep chasms.

I agree. Ruth believed in a different god from her mother-in-law. Naomi must have accepted Ruth for who she was, without attacking her religion, but she still told her about Jehovah, and finally Ruth received Naomi's God as her own Lord and Savior. I think one of the mistakes I make when I'm with someone who doesn't believe quite the same way as I do is to set about tearing down her theology instead of looking for some common ground. I should try to respect her beliefs.

To major on the majors and not on the minors?

Right. People's beliefs are very important to them. You can run into more conflict discussing religion than almost any other subject.

Religion or politics!

Religion or politics! Even evangelical Christians find lots to argue about.

Even mothers and daughters do! You and I had our problems over reading the Bible and praying! I remember one situation in particular. I was quite young and you tried to force me to have a quiet time every day. Because of the stage I was going through, I didn't feel like having regular devotions. So I told you that if you nagged me one more time, I'd never read the Bible again. Obviously, I wasn't serious. I suppose I was trying to say, "Jesus is real to me, Mom, but He shows Himself to me in different ways than He shows Himself to you." I had to find the reality of Christ for myself.

Oh, but I thought you were serious! I'll never forget the shock to my system the day you told me that! I closed your bedroom door very quietly, flew downstairs, fell on my knees and began to plead with God to forgive me, forgive you, and mend the mess I'd made. I decided then and there I had blown my parenting responsibility so badly that nothing would rectify the situation. "She'll run away from home, go on drugs, and die in a dark alley!" I wailed in my dramatic way. It seemed the Lord told me to quit squawking and listen to Him.

Mother! I'd no idea you took me so seriously. I never meant those sharp things I said. I just wanted you to get off my back.

I know that now; but it didn't help me then, because there was always the chance you did mean it. How is a mere mother expected to know?

So what did you do?

I stayed at my bedside a long time reading the New Testament and searching for comfort.

Knowing you, I bet you found some obscure verse that just fit!

How right you are! I read about Peter cutting the ear off the high priest's servant (see Luke 22:50). "There You are, Lord," I cried. "I've gone and cut Judy's spiritual ear off. Now she'll never listen to You again and it's all my fault!" Reading on, I noticed Jesus put the man's ear back again. That helped!

Mother, you're amazing! I'm sure I'd never have expressed myself so freely if I had known what was going on downstairs!

I needed to relax, let you grow up, and find a way to give God space to work in your life—to touch your ears in His time.

He did get my attention, you know. Many times He demonstrated His love for me by answering my prayers. I was petrified to go to a new school when we moved from England. On that first dreaded day, I turned to God and asked Him for two things. "Please give me peace so that I won't be scared to go to this big school where I don't know anybody," I pleaded, "and give me one or two special friends." God gave me everything I asked for. When I went to school, I wasn't the least bit nervous or scared. In fact, I was excited. Maybe I should have shared some of these things with you so you wouldn't have been so frightened.

You did tell me about the friends, but I didn't know you were so petrified about school.

He taught me that He was just as real to me as He was to you. I learned to go directly to Him with my problems, instead of via my mother, and He would be there to supply my every need.

I never realized how hard it must have been for you to find reality to your faith. Oh, I guess I recognized it would be a different thing from my black-and-white conversion, but I became impatient with the gray feeling you had about your Christianity. I had to give you permission to come to Christ in your own time instead of setting the spiritual alarm to go off. It was hard for me not to nag. Someone once told me that nagging was unforgiveness showing. I had to learn to forgive you for coming to Christ the way you wanted to.

Part of that is just the generation gap.

But age difference didn't give me permission to be close-minded to your way of doing things.

That's true. Even though Naomi and Ruth had differences concerning their religion, they were obviously open-minded enough to at least listen to each other's views.

That's unusual! Older people find it so much harder to make concessions and adjustments than younger people do. They get so set in their ways.

Like always harping back to the "good old days"?

Right.

Were the good old days really as good as you say they were, Mom, or does distance lend enchantment to the view?

Oh, I'm sure distance lends some enchantment, but I do think some things bear preserving. For example, dating customs have changed with the passing of time, and I'm not at all sure the changes are for the better.

I knew you were going to get to that!

Well, in my day, for example, the boy always asked the girl out. Not so now. Usually I brought a new boyfriend to the house to have a meal with my family on the very first date.

Did you really?

And we usually went out in groups rather than splitting off in twos and, what's more, we never kissed on the first few dates!

Well, it's sure different today! I guess it must have been hard for you to accept the American dating system. I just thought you were being awkward!

I had to try to adapt my old guidelines to a new rulebook I'd never read and seemed to vary depending on whom I asked!

I was coming from the opposite perspective. Because I spent my teenage years in the States, I naturally accepted things the way they were here. I had to try to understand the confusion you were experiencing and accept some rules that other girls my age didn't have to obey.

Which ones are you talking about?

Well, for example, when I first started dating, you only let me go out twice a month. As I grew older, the number of dates per month increased. Also, I always had a curfew.

To be fair, that relaxed as you grew older.

That's true. But Mom, most girls I hung around with never had a curfew! It was embarrassing to have to leave a party early. You gave me such a long list of don'ts.

It wasn't *that* long, but I do remember some of them. One forbade you to go to drive-in movies.

Normally, I was able to accept these guidelines, but we had some conflicts over them. When we didn't sit down and talk about the issues as they arose, the small rifts would turn into huge valleys that would be almost impossible to bridge later on. One particular situation would have become a major problem if we hadn't discussed it when it happened.

Oh dear, I think I know what you're going to say next.

I'm sure you do! When I would return home from a date and sit in the car talking for a few minutes, you would crawl over the plants in the bay window to peer at the car.

I could never see anything because you always parked conveniently behind the tree!

So then you'd put Plan B into action and start flickering the outside lights on and off. I was so embarrassed! One night after this happened, we sat down and talked about it and were able to reach a compromise that pleased both of us. Do you remember what we decided?

Yes, I do. You promised to bring your date inside to talk, and I agreed to leave you alone as long as it wasn't past your curfew. I suppose it all boils down to being determined to build a relationship.

To get back to our story, did you notice that Naomi recognized this same quality in Ruth? "When Naomi realized that Ruth was determined to go with her, she stopped urging her" (Ruth 1:18).

It's going to take steadfast determination to grow a solid love relationship. We've got to stick with it. That reminds me of the marriage relationship again. The Bible says we have to leave and cleave. The word *cleave* means to "stick to," like glue. The cement that will stick two people together is the steadfast determination to love and care when all that is left between the parties is the memory of that initial commitment. A "that's that" initial promise means working out the "what's what" of the problems at the nitty-gritty level.

We need to think of a good nitty-gritty example here. Let's talk about some of our fights. I lost my temper and said all sorts of things I later regretted—this tongue of mine—but you waited the fight out, you didn't come into the ring with me.

That's a good example. Because we had committed ourselves to a "that's that" relationship, what we said to each other, however hard, couldn't destroy it. We knew we were stuck with each other. It was at times like that, when you lashed out, I learned to ride out the storm. Just as you needed to stick with me when I got mad. I think you knew words wouldn't finish our friendship, didn't you?

There was always that marvelous security. Maybe I abused it, but I think that was because I was so sure of you. I guess I must have known it was safe to let fly—that nothing I could say would torpedo what we had going between us—or I wouldn't have dared to say half the things I did.

I can't help thinking about Ruth and Naomi. Naomi was a bitter, old woman at this point. What a challenge to see how a loving friendship changed a bitter woman into a better woman!

I think that thought belongs in chapter 3, Mom. We could do something on mending relationships next. Something really practical.

Fine. I think we've got our point across. Choosing involves commitment, which can be defined as a promise to another of a "that's that" forever relationship. Working it out will involve a sticky determination to see it through whatever the weather, rain, hail, or sun.

We have to be sure that what we find out about each other will not jeopardize our commitment. This gives both parties freedom to say anything they want to while they're working at understanding their differences.

Identification is putting ourselves at risk to find out what the other person thinks. That works only when we force ourselves to take initiatives. We need to be the first to ask questions, to find out something we can respect the other person for.

And it's being a Christian that motivates us to work that hard.

Right! I can remember treating people very shoddily before I came to Christ. When I'd get fed up with a relationship, I'd "can" it.

Just like that?

Just like that. Sometimes I'd have to lie my way out of it or manipulate the situation so I didn't look as bad as I undoubtedly was, but there was no sense of integrity, of trying to save my friendships. I sort of used people, I'm ashamed to say.

So what happened after your conversion? Did you feel obliged to work at all your relationships?

Yes, I really did, although there's a limit to the number of people you can be close to. Jesus had seventy friends, twelve good ones, and an inner circle of three. He even had one best friend. I guess that's a good pattern. I think the Lord expects us to work very hard with the twelve and be as loyal as time allows with the seventy. Think of it. Jesus intended us to be very serious about those who are close to us. He said, "Greater love has no one than this, than to lay down one's life for his friends" (John 15:13, NKJV). Now, that's commitment—not discarding people when they've served your purposes, but being willing to lay down your very life for them, even when they've discarded you.

When you don't feel like it?

Right.

We're back to commitment being grounded in love aren't we? The love of God that the Holy Spirit sheds abroad in our hearts—when we belong (see Romans 5:5).

Yes, when we belong, and when we let Him give us the power to go on loving. Being concerned when no one's concerned with us. We must remember Jesus' name was love …

… and Jesus' name was commitment too!

Commitment carries care as a matter of course
That's because He knows burdens are inevitable—
when you're committed.

He's never surprised when the going gets tough—
when the night comes—
He knows day follows night, and He waits for the sunrise.

Commitment is always
there—
in the dark—
and in the light, too—

When death seems far away—someone else's nightmare.
When the day dawns, lending its light to despondence,
or when we celebrate life rather than endure suffering,
commitment stands guard—
knowing the day brings its own snares.

When you're having fun, commitment can be a real nuisance
calling your actions into debate
reminding you of past promises—
Shaming you into His arms!

Commitment is really love in disguise—
intent on blessing you—always.
Commitment—
is Christ on a cross,
refusing the gift of vinegar—
accepting the gift of our sin as His own.

I want to be like Him—
committed!

Talk Time

1. Give examples of strains on your family relationships when hard times have come.

2. Each share a problem you've struggled with caused by the generation gap.

3. 1 Corinthians 13 defines God's agape love. Read it below. Circle the aspect of love that you find hardest to put into practice. Discuss.

4. Love is patient, love is kind. It does not envy, it does not boast, it is not proud. It is not rude, it is not self-seeking, it is not easily angered, it keeps no record of wrongs. Love does not delight in evil but rejoices with the truth (1 Corinthians 13:4–6).

5. What sort of quiet time is most meaningful/least meaningful to each of you? Why?

6. Do you judge each other's spirituality? Are you always taking each other's spiritual temperature? Each share an experience when God has made Himself real to you.

7. Choose one thing you need to be steadfastly determined to stick with in your relationships and pray about it.

Love is Forgiveness

Life is littered with broken relationships. I think that's because people live their lives in the realm of their emotions.

If we feel like it, we'll mend a hurt?

Right. Broken relationships take so much time and effort to restore. People seldom have the energy to bother.

We keep coming back to the difference it makes when you are committed to Christ who is committed to restoring things.

It is sheer obedience that motivates me even to try to mend some relationships. It's tempting to stay in Moab and try to forget the people I have left behind in Bethlehem.

Distance helps you forget, too.

Oh, distance can be a great hindrance. I find myself hoping I'll never see some people again. But that's no answer either because you continue to see them in your mind's eye. I've noticed that if I just hope a bad situation will go away or time and distance will help me forget it, neither happens. I either relive the unpleasant episode over and over again in my imagination or dream about it! On the other hand, if I make an honest effort to put things right, an inner healing of these memories begins to take place.

I know what you mean. It sure is tempting to bury our bone of contention and hope that no interfering hound will come along and dig it up again!

Love seeks to put things right—God's love, that is. God's love has reconciliation written all over it.

Do you think it was Naomi's faith that motivated her to go back to Bethlehem?

It could have been. We only know she was brave enough to return to the place of failure and try to pick up the pieces.

That's what the Bible says—"So the two women went on until they came to Bethlehem" (Ruth 1:19a).

When the couple arrived, the townspeople thought they recognized Naomi and curiously asked the older woman if she could possibly be the same person who had left Bethlehem all those years ago. Naomi answered that it was indeed she, but she told the people not to call her by her real name—which meant "pleasant." Instead, she wanted to be called Mara, meaning "bitter." She explained that she had left Bethlehem full, but the Lord had dealt severely with her, and she was returning a bitter woman.

Bitter women have a hard time restoring relationships.

It's interesting to see that she didn't wait until she felt good before she made a move.

But, then, bitterness seldom makes a move. It hardly retraces its steps. It rather stays entrenched in the slough of despondency, expecting others to make all the overtures. Naomi took the initiative and refused to allow her feelings to stop her.

When Grandma lived with us after discovering yet another cancer, I knew our relationship had to be healthy if we were going to help her through the last days of her life. You know, Judy, I felt so guilty because I really didn't want Grandma to die in our home. I was concerned about you kids watching that sort of intense suffering, and I was worried about handling the nursing involved. I prayed and prayed to God to make me want to have Grandma stay with us, but even after all the praying, I still felt the same. I knew I should say to her, "Mary, I want you to stay here so we can look after you," but I couldn't imagine using those words without meaning them. "That would be hypocrisy," I said to myself. I decided I would wait until Jesus made me want to say it.

Eventually it dawned on me that I had better speak to her before the feelings arrived in my heart—in case they never arrived at all! "Oh, God," I found myself praying, "don't let her know how I really feel." And so I talked to her, and her grateful response made me even more ashamed of myself. Weeks later, I suddenly realized how acceptable the whole situation had become. It's a question of doing the right things, not feeling the right thing.

Ruth did the right thing, too. It must have been extremely hard for her, yet she was determined to show Naomi friendship regardless of the consequences. It's that sort of love that changes a bitter woman into a better one. I can't help wondering if that occurred shortly after the two arrived in Bethlehem, because Naomi was never referred to as Mara again.

We really don't know the time frame, but what strikes me is that Naomi was as determined as Ruth to work at redeeming her relationships. When Naomi left Bethlehem with her family, she broke many of her ties. Obviously, some friendships disintegrated because of distance.

And I'm sure some of them ended because the townspeople couldn't understand why Naomi would leave a "blessed" place for a "blighted" one. The hometown folks must have felt rejected and hurt, and therefore would have decided it was quite legitimate to sever their connections with Naomi.

That's a good point, Judy. When Naomi returned to Bethlehem, she had to face those very people!

I'm sure the mending process took quite a long time, but I believe Naomi succeeded.

I'm sure she did, too. A reconciliation had obviously taken place by the time Ruth gave birth to Obed, because chapter 4:14–17 says that the women gathered around Naomi. In other words, they shared in her joy.

I wonder if Ruth kept in touch with her own people? Don't you think that her folk must have felt a bit rejected too?

We really don't know. I'm tempted to think that she probably had a harder time living with her memories than Naomi did.

What do you mean?

As far as we know, Ruth didn't have the opportunity to go back to Moab in person. Everything would have had to have been achieved long distance. Have you ever tried to fix a broken relationship that way? It's hard …

… and extremely frustrating! You can't even see the other person's nonverbal reactions. All you have to go by is the sound of a voice on the telephone or the tone of a letter. There was no fax or e-mail either. Poor Ruth didn't even have a cell phone. I can't imagine living without that!

Me neither, although Dad could live without the bills! What a modern miracle it is to be able to pick up a piece of plastic and talk to each other! How many times did we use that link when issues weren't fully resolved between us?

Many times! When Greg was living in Evanston and I was still in Wheaton, I spent as many weekends as possible with him planning our wedding. One time you and Dad stopped by for dinner, do you remember? All through the meal I knew you were dying to ask me what the sleeping arrangements were, but you didn't interrogate us. After you left, I felt so happy. Your silence proved you trusted me.

Greg and I knew that it was very important where we slept. This could be a witness to all our non-Christian friends. So we had already decided that Greg would sleep on the floor in the basement of our building and I would stay in the apartment. Because you hadn't asked me about the issue, I wanted you to know what we had decided. I waited until I knew you would be home and then used that little bit of plastic to call and tell you not to worry.

When Dad and I got in the car after spending the evening with you, he turned to me and said, "Well done, Jill, you kept your mouth shut!" I must admit I felt very proud of myself. It had been so hard to stop sneaking looks around Greg's apartment to try to figure out if there was a spare bed! You'll never know what a joy it was when you called us at midnight to tell us what you had worked out. That saved me from a sleepless night!

Even with the telephone, it still took a long time to solve some of our conflicts, didn't it?

Yes, but that's where commitment comes in—the commitment to keep on trying.

When you wonder if you'll ever arrive at some common ground with someone, don't give up because success could be just around the corner!

What happens when success isn't just around the corner? The problem is that you don't know what will happen when you reach out to someone who has been offended. She might reject you and send you running back to Moab!

If she rejects you, you've done your part. You've tried.

When something has come between one of my friends and me, I go about my daily duties with a huge sense of apprehension. It's horrible—like a damp cloak. But the feeling lifts when I deliberately begin to make a move toward the hurt party—even without any assurance of a positive response at the end of the line.

Shortly after we arrived in America and had begun our ministry at the church, I became aware of a woman in our congregation who appeared hurt and angry with me. I didn't even know her name. I couldn't imagine why she was upset, and I didn't want to find out either! I hoped she would get over whatever it was that was bugging her without a confrontation. I avoided her by the simple expedient of noticing where she sat in church and sitting on the opposite side of the sanctuary. Then one day I bumped into her in the local supermarket. Turning a corner by the breads, I caught sight of her at the other end of the aisle by the cereals. I had an instant choice to make. "To face or not to face"—that was the question. I had to make up my mind whether I was going to retreat behind the dog food or deliberately meet her halfway by the cake mixes and say something. "But what would I say?" I wondered. Coming to a decision, I approached the offended woman. There was no time to compose a speech. I noticed with some relief that she looked as apprehensive as I felt. So, as our carts met, I blurted out, "I have no idea what I have done to offend you, but I am very sorry." To my amazement, after an embarrassing silence, she offered some sort of apology and without ever telling me what the problem had been, passed by the paper products on her way to the fruit and vegetables. Neither of us knew how the other would react in that particular situation, but we both walked across the no-man's-land of wondering and faced each other.

In the end, misunderstandings have to be tackled. We all need to return to the place of failure and the people we have failed or who have failed us, and seek to make amends. They call it confrontation—facing up to faces after a face off!

Don't you think the reason a lot of people don't deal with their broken relationships is because of pride? I know pride has stopped me from saying I'm sorry to my family.

I remember one particular situation when you were glad you swallowed your pride.

You mean when Greg and I had a huge fight and "broke up"?

Yes.

As you know, I have a wicked tongue and didn't hesitate to use it to speak my mind before I turned and walked away from him. After I'd covered about a quarter of a mile, I began to think. One part of me wanted to keep going—happy that I had had the final say. But the other part of me realized that if I didn't go back and apologize, I might never have the opportunity again. After a while, I turned and went back. That was one of the hardest things I have ever done.

It was Christ who finally turned me around. As Christians, we are supposed to be Christlike. Because Christ hates pride, we should hate pride too. We are told to love one another, and love is not proud.

Exactly. Even though it is hard, we have to ask God to help us and He will. All too often I would much rather play a game of make-believe that the quarrel never happened than admit my part.

Naomi wasn't proud. She and Elimelech had demonstrated an independent spirit in forsaking Bethlehem in the first place, especially after

God had clearly indicated His hand was upon the town and its inhabitants. Perhaps Elimelech couldn't find the faith to wait out adversity with the people of God. Who knows what hard things were said to the family as they packed up and took off. It must have taken an awful lot of humility to return.

One of the hardest things to face up to is failure—to be expected to show great faith and blow it, and then have to crawl back and admit it. I remember a spell in the hospital when I was terrified of the anesthetic. I felt so ashamed when the nurses noticed my panic. It was awful to have to come back from surgery to the same faces after I had wanted to be such an example. I had to learn to tell people I'd failed and say, "I'm not perfect. I get scared just like you!"

That was what Naomi did, wasn't it? She bravely went back to Bethlehem and began honestly to face up to the people she had left behind. "I'm bitter," she said! She was able to tell them that she and Elimelech had stepped out of the will of God, and they had made things very difficult for themselves because of it. She admitted their part in the mistake.

That's always a great place to start! When you are trying to mend a hurt, it's a good idea to begin by admitting your wrong. Naomi didn't say to the women of Bethlehem, "Why didn't you stop us from leaving? It's all your fault!" Instead she told them what had happened to the family without laying blame on anyone else's door!

She didn't blame God for it either. Sometimes we are bitter at God for allowing us to have our willful way. I think Naomi was bitter at herself.

That's very important. Why people blame God for the repercussions of their own stupidity, I'll never know, but they do.

Naomi was able to say, "Look, it's been really tough going, but the Lord has been dealing with me. I've learned many lessons along the way." That's a great thing to do when you are confronting someone. Share some of the things God has been teaching you in Moab, because people can relate to that. Everyone has spent part of his life in the far country!

Like the prodigal son. Jesus told a story about a wealthy boy who had everything going for him. He took off for a far country where he spent his inheritance and finished up so poverty-stricken that he had to feed pigs. Finally he "came to himself" and said,

" 'How many of my father's hired servants have food to spare, here I am starving to death! I will set out and go back to my father, and will say to him: Father, I have sinned against heaven and against you. I am no longer worthy to be called your son; make me like one of your hired men.'" (Luke 15:17–19).

If we want to, we can sit in a pigsty of self-pity forever. God allows us that privilege, but how much better to take the long road back to a loving Father who will run to meet us once we have set out for Bethlehem.

But what about the unloving brother he had left behind? The older man who stayed at home didn't respond positively to the return of the prodigal. In fact, he was quite offended at all the fuss!

Right. Naomi fared better, although I bet she had her share of "older sisters" waiting for her back at the ranch. Jesus' parable had the right idea. The prodigal son admitted his faults and returned home a better man for the hard lessons he'd learned.

You can always find something of spiritual value to share from a hard experience. This way you don't put people on the defensive. Of course, you may find only one party is willing to dialogue, as in the case of the prodigal son and his brother. Then what do you do?

You try to stay within reach. Give it time so you can show the people you've hurt that you really want to be part of their lives again. Naomi could have come back, tried to make things right, found the people unhelpful, and returned to Moab.

How do we know the townspeople of Bethlehem were unhelpful?

Well, we know Elimelech's family still lived in Bethlehem and therefore could have alleviated much of Ruth and Naomi's physical distress. But they didn't appear to help them. Ruth was forced to go out and find work.

And yet there is no record of Naomi harboring a grudge against her relatives.

No, I'm sure she didn't. Of course, you can't talk about mending relationships without mentioning forgiveness. I believe Naomi forgave the people, but she probably took a little time forgiving herself.

That's my problem. When I experience a broken relationship, I usually blame myself for it. Then I have a hard time getting rid of my guilt!

There are always two sides to every story. That's the thing we need to remember when we become busy apportioning blame. I think when you've done your part and tried to put things right, you have to let it rest and get on with life.

Have you always managed to put things right, Mom?

I wish! I'm rather a coward about it. I hate to confront anyone in case I learn something about myself I can't handle.

We have to get back to the basics again, don't we? We should ask for forgiveness because we're told to—not because we want to—and we must do it because loving Jesus means being obedient. Paul said "... even as Christ forgave you, so you also must do" (Colossians 3:13, NKJV).

"As" is a pretty big word! We have to ask ourselves, "How did He forgive me? If I don't know that, then I won't know how to forgive others."

He gave freely for a start. He didn't charge us for it.

How could we ever repay Him for forgiving us? What currency would we use? Once Dad and I were working with street gangs in Europe, and a few of the wildest youngsters asked us if we would take them to church. We complied with some trepidation, realizing the visit would be a first for most of them.

When the time came for the collection plate to be passed along the row, the lads couldn't believe their good fortune. Here was a plateful of money being invitingly passed under their very noses! They did the obvious thing and helped themselves. By the time the plate reached the hands of the horrified ushers, it was clean! After the service, I returned as much of the offering as I could, explaining that the idea was to give our money to God. "Wot does 'e need it for?" inquired an astonished teenager, not irreverently. "Didn't you tell us forgiveness was free?" I'll never forget that experience, for more reasons than the obvious one!

I think some churchgoers today think they are somehow paying their passage to heaven by way of the collection plate.

Or by their church attendance or good deeds. The lads off the street certainly had the right idea. God gives. All we paupers can do is to take thankfully. God's forgiveness is free! What's more, He forgave fully, He didn't say, "I forgive you everything *except* this or that."

He forgave forever too. He's not going to suddenly expose our secret sins one day.

That's incredible grace. When I think of people I've fallen out with, I don't forgive them freely and fully like God. I like to reserve some of the hurtful memories to play with. In fact, I almost relish the thought of cornering them one day and saying, "Aha, you thought you'd gotten away with it, didn't you? Well, now you'll have to face up to it and pay your dues!"

Jesus forgave so many people so many things.

Yes, He did. Then He forgot it!

Now that's the hardest part! It reminds me of the story Dad tells about when he visited the African witch doctor. He went into the witch doctor's mud hut and noticed that the man had all sorts of objects hanging from the roof of his home. Dad asked the witch doctor about the items. Do you remember what the man said?

Yes, he said that each object represented a person who had done something to him or one of his family members. The reminders hung from the ceiling so that he would be sure to see them every morning when he got up and every night when he went to bed. That way he would never forget to hate his enemies for what they had done.

Isn't that sad? Instead of being willing to forget, this man was willing to remember. Greg and I have a pact. If we are fighting at bedtime, we won't go to bed mad at each other. Obviously, our fights can't always be solved before we retire, so sometimes we have to go to sleep agreeing to disagree. Then, when there's plenty of time and we're both fresh, we talk about the whole situation.

In other words, you adhere to Ephesians 4:26: "… do not let the sun go down while you are still angry."

Exactly.

I counseled a woman who had come to me with a truly horrific account of abuse. She described her days as a nightmare; her nights were like a horror film. She would dread her husband's coming home from a drinking spree, which he did with monotonous regularity, and she gave me a blow-by-blow description of the gory events that followed. He particularly enjoyed whipping her with a wet towel and slapping her face till her eyes closed with the bruisings so she wouldn't see him drunk— seeing it upset her so much.

But as I listened intently to the woman's story, I began to have questions about the truth of it. Her face, though pale and fragile, bore no signs of the fighting she related. And yet her graphic retelling of the terrible battering she received was so vivid I was sure she must have left her husband standing at the door of her house with the wet towel swinging in his hand.

I began to try to verify her testimony and discovered the abuse had occurred more than fifteen years ago. She had not been able to forgive it and therefore had not been able to forget it! In fact, she had been deliberately bringing it all to mind daily, so that that very morning she had relived the horror of it all over again. I was able to tell her she needed to let Jesus reach up with His nail-pierced hand and take down all those photographs that were hanging around the roof of her mind as surely as those objects hung around the witch doctor's hut! If only the woman in question had made a pact with her husband, as you and Greg did at the start of your marriage, it might have been different.

I think only Christ can help us to forgive and forget the terrible things that happen. Corrie ten Boom, who spent time in a concentration camp, tells a story about forgiving a prison guard. One evening, at the conclusion of one of her meetings, a man walked up to her and thanked her for the message she had given. He went on to express his gratitude to God for forgiving his sins. Then he held out his hand to Corrie. She couldn't move. She recognized him as one of the SS men who had stood guard at the shower-room door at Ravensbruck. She could still vividly remember the guards' laughs and jeers as she and the prisoners walked past them naked. She knew that she needed to forgive him, but she couldn't. Finally, she prayed that Jesus would give her His forgiveness for the man. All of a sudden, Corrie was able to shake hands with him. She learned that we have to ask Jesus for His forgiveness to forgive our friends and enemies, and He will give it to us.[1]

We need to master the same lesson. If she was able to forgive that former guard after all he had put her through, then we can learn to forgive others for what they have done to us. For example, husbands and wives need to start forgiving each other. I don't mean saying the words "I forgive you" and then continuing on the same way as before. Instead, say and show forgiveness; prove it with actions. A pretty woman I was counseling in Australia was struggling with this very concept. She discovered that her husband had committed adultery. Finally, after much grief and anguish, she was able to go before God and forgive her husband for what he had done. Of course, that was extremely difficult for her to do, but it wasn't her hardest task. She knew that even though she had prayed about it, she now had to get into bed with him. That's real forgiveness.

When I was in high school, you demonstrated the same principle with acts of kindness. It seemed that the bigger the brat I was, the more you would try to kill me with kindness, as if to say, "Judy, I forgive you for what you're doing, and instead of just telling you that I do, I'm going to show you."

Do you really remember those times? I'm glad, because sometimes I thought I'd never get through to you.

I was just too stubborn to thank you for all you did for me. I felt so guilty because I was mean to you, and yet you always returned my animosity with kindness. That was the best thing you could have done to mend our fragile relationship. I know I probably never told you this when we'd make up, but it was always your actions that got through. Actions do speak louder than words!

God's sort of love is actively kind. Kindness is the active part of patience. Love suffers long and is kind while it's waiting out the suffering situation. But it wasn't always a one-way street, Judy. You were kind to me, too. One thing I really appreciated was your quickness to forgive and forget. In fact, I often went to bed and fretted the long hours of the night away about some show of anger or impatience on my part, and you got up in the morning and greeted me as if it had never happened!

Sometimes I was just pretending I'd forgotten. I still felt resentful, but I knew my behavior had to be right.

If only we could learn that hardest of lessons. We must act in kindness before our feelings catch up with us.

I think one of the most difficult things for me to do after I've told someone I've forgiven them is to try to restore the relationship right away. As you said, Mom, sometimes the feelings aren't there when you need them. When I was very young, I had an argument with Dad. After it was all over, and we had both said we were sorry, he told me to give him a kiss. I didn't want to! I had forgiven him, yet my feelings hadn't caught up with my words.

What happened?

I kissed him. I guess I knew that I needed to restore the relationship even if I didn't feel like it. You're right about Naomi being a good example of this principle. Even though she was a bitter woman, when she returned to Bethlehem, she didn't withdraw from society and disappear.

It's great therapy to face the root cause of bitterness and deal with it actively. Otherwise that bitter root invades everything. It infects our minds and souls. It doesn't do us any good at all. Naomi knew that.

Bitterness is like the plague. I read about a family who lived in London during the great plague. The death carts came around the streets every morning to collect the corpses. One family fled to a town at the other end of the country to escape the carnage. They didn't know the plague was in their clothing. They died, and so did thousands of other innocent people who caught the disease from them.

People try to get over their bitterness by moving out of town, changing their jobs, or trying to get away from an offending relative. But bitterness has no problem keeping pace with our fleeing feet. It must be faced, repented of, and renounced, or we will end up infecting others.

Any handy hints on how to start?

We can begin by keeping short accounts with God. Don't let sin pile up or solidify into cold, settled hatred. Confess it. This habit can help us to start and keep short accounts with people, too.

And if there is no response?

Then you have to forgive the person for not responding.

As Naomi must have had to do?

Yes. But, then, Naomi knew what it was to love.

Love always overcomes bitterness,
regardless of how love feels,
despite manifold reasons
to harbor a grudge—
Love works at forgiving,
rising early
looking for the hurt one,
chasing down the wounded,
binding up the hurts with words of reconciliation.
Love retires late, tired with trying
to make amends,
sleeping swiftly
eager to rise and begin again.
Love never gives up.
Love that gives up—
isn't love.

Talk Time

1. Do you wait until you feel like it to tell each other you are sorry? Discuss.

2. Do you find it hard to admit you are wrong? Read Luke 18:9–14. Which of the characters do you most readily identify with?

3. Match the principle with the corresponding verse.

   Jesus forgave forever.   Isaiah 55:7
   Jesus forgave freely.   1 John 1:9
   Jesus forgave fully.   Isaiah 43:25

4. Is there something you need to forgive someone for? Discuss.

5. Pray about it together.

Love Nourishes

Now we get into the romantic bit. What a love story! After Naomi and Ruth had settled down in Bethlehem, Ruth began to search for work. Gleaning laws in the Old Testament had made marvelous provision for the poor and the strangers who lived among the Israelites, and Ruth knew the rich landowners would leave grain in the corners of their fields for unfortunate people like herself. She made up her mind to follow behind the reapers, hoping they would be generous. In a master understatement, the Bible tells us, "… her hap was to light on a part of the field belonging unto Boaz, who was the kindred of Elimelech" (Ruth 2:3 KJV). Oh, the happy "haps" of God! She just "hap" to light on a portion of Boaz's field— a man who was actually a relative of Naomi. There is nothing "hap" hazard about God's plans and purposes. Relationships planned by God don't just happen to hap! Someone is standing in the shadows, orchestrating the divine details. If only we would leave the meeting place to God, there might be more forever love stories!

That's true, Mom. But sometimes it isn't that easy. When I was growing up, you told me that God had the right man already picked out for me, but I still worried that we would both arrive in the same field at the same time.

You shouldn't have worried.

You're right. When I look back on how Greg and I met, I know it was one of God's "happy happenings." I was a freshman at Wheaton, in premed and terrified of failing, so I spent every possible minute studying. One Monday morning, I was in the library reviewing chemistry. Someone pulled out the chair to the carrel next to mine and sat down. I didn't bother to look up, because I presumed it wasn't anyone I'd know. After a few minutes, I had this strange feeling that someone was staring at me, so I glanced up and saw this gorgeous blond-haired guy sitting sideways in his chair waiting patiently to talk with me. I was so embarrassed, I didn't know what to say or do. I had no idea that this perfect stranger would one day become my husband.

It was exciting to see how that happening happened. For years, God had been preparing both of you separately so that you would choose to attend Wheaton and meet in the library!

It's true. If we'll only trust the Lord with our little lists of what we'd like for a husband, He will provide for us. Of course, this doesn't always mean He'll give us everything we ask for, but He will take care of us whether we marry or not. Didn't you ever worry about meeting your Boaz?

Yes, I did. But I didn't doubt God's ability to bring us together. I doubted me! I always believed He would get the man of my dreams to Boaz's field, but I wondered if I would be there when he arrived! I used to play "what if" games. What if I was out of touch with God when Boaz appeared? Or what if he was out of touch with God when I appeared? Or, then again, what if both of us were out of touch and no one appeared! The permutations seemed interminable. Eventually I learned to channel my energies toward more productive pursuits and tried to keep my mind busy with serving the Lord, trusting Him with the meeting plans.

The most important thing is to know what sort of man you are looking for in the first place, so that you will recognize him when he does come along.

Boaz certainly recognized a good thing when he saw it. Visiting his property to see how the reapers were reaping, he scanned the horizon and was stunned to see Ruth graciously gleaning her way through the fields toward him. In the prosaic language of the *King James Bible*, he asked his men, "Whose damsel is this?" (Ruth 2:5). Or, in the language of our day and age, he exclaimed, "Wow! Who's she?" The reapers responded with the appropriate information:

"It is the young Moabite woman who came back with Naomi from the country of Moab. And she said, 'Please let me glean and gather after the reapers among the sheaves.' So she came and has continued from morning until now …"

Then Boaz said to Ruth, "You will listen, my daughter, will you not? Do not go to glean in another field, nor go from here, but stay close by my young women" (vv. 6–8, NKJV).

Now, we know what he really meant was "stay by me," not "stay by my maidens." We don't need to be very clever to see the way the wind was blowing!

How romantic! I can just see Ruth bowing herself to the ground and saying, "Why have I found favor in your eyes, that you notice me, since I am a foreigner?" (v. 10).

The thing that interests me isn't what Ruth says at this point, but rather what Boaz says, because it shows me the sort of qualities he appreciated and perhaps the woman of character he had been searching for. Look at the words in verses 11 and 12. He commends Ruth for her courage in leaving her homeland and for her respect and commitment toward her mother-in-law. Above all, he encourages her in her newfound faith in Jehovah, "under whose wings you have come for refuge" (v. 12b).

That was important to him, wasn't it, that she trusted in Jehovah?

Yes, and rightly so. Couples have enough adjustments to make without bickering about their different religious beliefs. I think it's really important to sort that out before the marriage takes place.

I don't think Boaz would have married someone who didn't love Jehovah, do you?

No, I don't. I think he had the proper perspective on the issue. Ruth had not been brought up in his church so to speak, but she had come to trust his God and he knew that was the most important thing.

You and Dad always emphasized that.

How can two people be truly one when they cannot share the deepest part of themselves with each other?

Faith binds us together.

It's certainly the thing that I love most about Stuart. When I see how much he loves God, it makes me love him all the more because I love God so much!

Boaz was a man of faith—in fact, he sounds like the Proverbs 31 man to me.

He does a bit!

You and Dad told us kids to be really picky with our friends—especially those of the opposite sex. Once I asked you if I could go out with a certain boy and when you looked doubtful, I said, "He's a Christian, Mom." Whereupon you said, "But, Judy, it's not enough just to be a Christian.

What sort of a Christian is he?" You taught us to choose close friends with strong Christian convictions; to aim high when it came to our special relationships.

I know how easy it is to settle for just any relationship rather than the right one, to get impatient waiting, to be tempted to take things into your own hands. I remember listing all the qualities of the man of my dreams. He had to trust Jehovah, be a courageous and caring human being, and then I added a whole bunch of things I don't think Boaz had in mind when he was looking for a partner—things like tall, dark, and handsome, musical, sporty, and have a good sense of humor.

So what did you do once you'd finished writing your order?

I knelt down by my bed and read it out to God.

Did you think He was deaf or couldn't read English?

You know, Judy, it was silly, but I wanted to be sure He heard and understood all the details—the fine print. How stupid I was! As if He didn't read my innermost desires before I even had them! Anyway, I gave Him my order and then seemed to hear Him say to me, "Now, let me have the list!" That was a different thing altogether. To give Him my order was one thing, but to surrender my list was another! Why, if I let Him keep it, He might alter it, tear it up, or lose it! Anyway, I well remember the struggle that went on in that young, yearning, and romantic heart of mine. It took a long time before I gave Him permission to do what He willed with my dreams.

But, Mom, your story has a happy ending. God did bring along the man of your dreams. What about all the people who have made their lists and given them to Him, and He hasn't come through? There are so many Ruths that you and I know personally—beautiful, young, Christian women who have been gleaning in hard places all their lives without ever seeing Boaz on the horizon.

When you give Him the list, you give Him the privilege to decide your future for you. That's the point. You've got to come to the place of giving up *your* desires for His desires. I'm sure Ruth was not expecting a husband to appear.

That's so hard when you want to be married, don't you think?

Of course, it is awfully hard. I can remember praying fervently, "Lord, I am willing to give You the list and never be married." Oh, I said the words with as much sincerity as I could—loudly, many times, for added emphasis. I was hoping that the Lord would be so impressed with my prayer He would reward me by producing the desired husband immediately! He didn't. Instead, He brought me to a broader place, a spiritual honesty that whispered, "Lord, I'm *not* willing, but I'm willing to be made willing." Then He could work!

We don't know how long Boaz had been looking for his woman of character. We do believe he was much older than Ruth. I like to think he had decided if he couldn't find what he was looking for, he would do without! I wish we were such lookers, instead of panicking and settling for second best, which so often happens. But I understand it because being single seems like such a lonely state.

I used to consider it a punishment of sorts. Then I read 1 Corinthians 7 and discovered it was a privilege, not a punishment.

What do you mean?

Paul talked of the single person as being free to attend upon the Lord without distraction.

I don't know if the guys would like to be thought of as distractions!

I think Paul meant the married woman spends an awful lot of time thinking about how she can please her husband, while the single woman has no such conflict of interests.

But didn't God have marriage in mind as the "normal" thing?

He certainly ordained marriage and considers it a basic building block of society. It is used as a picture of Jehovah's relationship with Israel and Christ's relationship with His church.

But Jesus Himself was single.

He chose to be. And Paul said others may choose to remain so for many good reasons.

He said he would like to spare married people the sorrows of seeing their family suffer in the persecution that was beginning, and wished many were single as he. This way they could buy up spiritual opportunities in those difficult days.

But he also said both marriage and singleness are presents from God. We are not supposed to pout over the particular gift He has given us, but rather to explore the grand possibilities of both the married and single state.

Not seeking, but resting.

Not striving …

Conniving …

But rather, arriving at acceptance—a very peaceful place to be.

I'm sure both Ruth and Boaz had gotten to that point.

I'm sure, too.

It must have been such joy for them to discover God's wonderful surprise!

Once Boaz had been alerted to the possibility of a relationship with Ruth, he pursued it; he gave it time. Time is a great tester of character. Given time, masks fall off to reveal the real person underneath.

I'm very experienced at "time testing." Greg and I met in October of my freshman year. I had so much schooling ahead that we couldn't allow ourselves to become very serious about each other. At first we accomplished this by trying to keep our relationship casual, with no strings attached. But after a while, we realized that we wanted to spend more time with each other. During our first two summers, we were separated. Those months were very hard and yet extremely valuable. We decided that we were both free to date other people. Although neither of us really wanted to or rarely did, this freedom gave us time to reconsider our commitment to each other. When we returned in the fall, our relationship was stronger than when we had left in the spring.

I think one of the most reliable things that time gave you both was the opportunity to learn how to really communicate.

That's true. When Greg and I were students and had very little money, we spent many of our dates just sitting and talking. This may sound boring to some people, but it really wasn't. It gave me the chance to really get to know the man I was going to spend the rest of my life with.

Time is friendship's friend. Half the problem with marriages today is the lack of honest friendship. How can we really know each other if we only communicate on a sexual level? It takes time for our words to explain our hopes and fears to one another.

Well, time and words certainly made our friendship grow. Because we had to set strict boundaries around our sexual conduct, we did the things friends, rather than lovers, do.

I'll always remember the phone call you made to your dad—

When I asked him if I could marry my best friend?

Yes! It gave us great confidence that yours would be a marriage that would last. Friendship nourishes a relationship like nothing else does.

Well, Boaz had apparently taken lots of time and trouble to find out all he could about Ruth. Once he discovered what he had been looking for, he began to nourish the relationship.

You know, Mom, there are so many creative ways to do that. Boaz wanted to get to know Ruth better. He discovered that giving Ruth time, not things, deepened their love. Ruth was very poor and needed food, and Boaz could easily have given her a gift of barley. He was also in a position to give her money. Instead, he strategized that if he would be near her all day long, then he would be able to use mealtimes as an excuse to talk with her and get to know her better and he did just that.

Now Boaz said to her at mealtime, "Come here, and eat of the bread, and dip your piece of bread in the vinegar." So she sat beside the reapers, and he passed parched grain to her; and she ate and was satisfied ... (Ruth 2:14 NKJV).

Boaz was certainly very creative. I think he nourished their love to a far greater degree by giving Ruth himself in that way.

When we reached the age where we all had everything we needed, Christmas and birthdays became a hassle because we couldn't figure out what to give each other. Then you had a great idea. You decided we should start to give time, not things. All of our relationships grew to a new depth because we began to spend quality time together. For example, I think our family mealtimes have always been very special. We don't eat together very often, but when we do, everyone enjoys it. We all look forward to those reunions because they're one of the few chances we have to catch up on everyone else's news. In our family, there are always new jokes and plenty of laughter, too. But, do you know why I really look forward to our meals? It's because of the tradition we started a couple of years ago of ending those family times with fellowship.

It's so thrilling to hear how God has been taking care of each one of us and answering our prayers.

I don't think I'd know about everyone's struggles, defeats, and victories if it wasn't for that intimate time. I think the reason we all feel free to share is because we are in a familiar setting. Mealtime has been listening and talk time for years now. I have given us a lunch together for your birthday, Dad a pancake breakfast for Father's Day, and Pete a "dinner date" for Christmas. What wonderful opportunities to concentrate on getting to know one member of the family better!

It's interesting because I've found that each one of us has his own idea of how to do this. As you said, Judy, you buy us all meals together, whereas Peter gives us tickets to sports events. When Pete was fourteen, and it was "Ladies Day" at County Stadium, he asked me if I would like to go to the Brewers' game with him. Of course, I was thrilled. I was going to spend time with my youngest son!

Well, it was hysterical. We arrived at the stadium and had to stand in line for tickets. After a while, Pete told me to go and stand in the corner and wait for him there—he would get the tickets. I didn't know why he had asked me to do that until I looked around. Then I realized that all the other men had their girlfriends with them. Poor Pete was standing in line with his mother!

When we finally sat down, I realized it was freezing. Pete had to get up at least three times to go and buy me hot chocolate. In between the hot chocolate runs, we sat in dead silence watching the game. At one point, I decided that since this was our in-depth time together, we should be talking. So I racked my brain for an intelligent question about baseball and finally thought of one. From the pained look on Pete's face, I determined it hadn't been a very good question after all.

Even if you didn't talk much, at least you were together. I think it's special that a fourteen-year-old boy would even ask his mom to go to a baseball game with him, don't you?

Oh yes, although I've noticed that he's never invited me again! Obviously I was excited to spend whatever time I could with Pete during his teenage years. It's harder for a mom to think of special things to do with a teenage son than it is with a daughter. Do you remember Dad and I giving you and Dave tickets to *Romeo and Juliet* when you were about ages twelve and thirteen?

I sure do. We had to get all dressed up and go to the play. It was good for both of us because we would never have chosen to do that sort of thing on our own.

Did you enjoy it?

Well, I thought it was OK. Dave said that he couldn't understand the funny language the actors and actresses were using.

That hurts! They were speaking in Shakespearean English! Oh well, I suppose that's one of the prices we have paid in moving to America!

I think the best example we could give was what you did for our twenty-fifth wedding anniversary.

When the boys came and asked me what we should do for you and Dad, we had a big problem thinking of something. We knew you didn't want a party, seeing as you are both peopled out most of the time. Anyway, we didn't know who to ask and who to leave out without offending someone.

So you came up with the neat idea of giving us two days in a nice hotel at a resort center so we could get away and be alone!

After we'd made all the plans, it looked so exciting that I said to the boys, "Why should they have all the fun? Why don't we all go along!"

And you did. And we loved it! All of us piled into that super room together celebrating twenty-five years of marriage and family—

—and relationships!

Exactly. Relationships that we had tried to nourish through the years with creative care. I think we parents need to do more to remind our children to do such things for each other. I know I have constantly told one or another of you kids that a birthday card, a visit while in college, a packet of home-baked cookies, or a telephone chat would be appreciated. Somehow it takes a little time before the idea catches on.

Nourishing is a learned art, and learning presupposes teaching. And part of teaching is reminding people of what they have already learned! I used to feel hurt when my brothers had to be reminded to get me a birthday card, but I know now they never forgot to love me, they just forgot to tell me!

We should all help each other to remember to tell our love in some creative or concrete way. I know I've been helped when someone has reminded me about a birthday or anniversary that has slipped my mind. I heard about a mother who provided calendars at Christmastime for all of her family. She put everybody's birthday, graduation, and anniversary dates on it. For an hour's worth of work, it saved an awful lot of hurt feelings!

Good idea—you should do that for us, Mom!

Not only did Boaz think of creative ways to nourish his relationship with Ruth, he thought of practical ways, too. Boaz told his reapers to allow Ruth to glean in areas that were beyond the edges of the field, and he also suggested that they drop a little extra barley here and there for Ruth. "Let her glean even among the sheaves, and do not reproach her. Also let some grain from the bundles fall purposely for her; leave it that she may glean. ..." (Ruth 2:15–16, NKJV).

Boaz wasn't the only person working on his interpersonal relationships. Ruth was busy too. Because Ruth was a stranger in town, she could have insisted that Naomi go and work among her own people while she, Ruth, stayed home. But we don't see her acting that way. She realized that one practical way to show her love for Naomi would be to go out and get a job. "So Ruth the Moabitess said to Naomi, 'Please let me go to the field, and glean heads of grain after him in whose sight I may find favor'" (Ruth 2:2, NKJV).

That's a good example for all of us. In-law relationships are a great place to practice practical love. When Greg was living with us the summer before you two got married, he built our beautiful, brick patio. Everyday I'd see him out there hammering those bricks into place, and I would experience a grateful sense of appreciation for his careful effort. The project gave us time to talk and laugh and afforded me a chance to appreciate his clever workmanship. He's such a handyman, Judy! Practical love says more than impractical words can ever say, however beautifully they are couched. At the end of that project, I took that young man of yours out for a pancake breakfast. Just him and me! I told him over the waffles laden with sticky strawberries and foamy cream that I appreciated his work, but more importantly I appreciated him! I was able to say—shyly I remember, but with utmost sincerity—"Thank you for not only walking into Judy's life but into mine as well!" That whole thing was a significant factor in the deepening of our relationship.

Mom, you did many practical things for me, too. Do you remember how clothes-conscious I was when I was in high school? Every night before I went to bed, I'd spend half an hour deciding what I'd wear the next day. One night I couldn't find the blouse that I wanted. Finally I figured out that it must be in the laundry, so I flew down to the basement to see if it had been washed. Just as I reached the bottom of the stairs, you came in the front door. You had been away at some meetings and looked exhausted. But because I was preoccupied with myself in those days, I didn't stop to consider your state before I asked you to go downstairs, find my blouse, and wash it for me. You did it without even saying, "Wait a minute until I catch my breath."

But lest anyone think me a Proverbs 31 woman, Judy, I would have to add in all honesty that I probably spoiled you kids. My motive was not always that of love! I suppose I had a real fear that you would resent my ministry or the Lord Himself if I left you too much work to do while I was out of the house serving Him. So I went an extra mile or two to make sure everything was in order, cooked up, washed up, and lined up before I left! Being away put a big load on you, Judy, and I didn't want to see you go under, so I tried to do things that I probably wouldn't have done if I'd been home all the time. But in the doing of those concrete things, I couldn't help but notice the effectiveness of practical love. Your emotions were touched far more by my washing your blouse for you at 10:30 P.M. than they would have been by my saying, "Judy, I love you. Wash your own blouse!" Practical acts of love nourished our relationship in a very concrete way. But then, love in the abstract is easy. It's love in the concrete that's hard—if you'll excuse the pun!

I'll excuse it, Mom!

If we're talking about being practical, what about all you did for me in Australia?

Practical love can be hard work! You had just damaged your back and had been ordered six weeks of bed rest. But instead of staying flat on your back, you spent five weeks traveling in airplanes and cars on a ministry tour. I was supposed to be your companion, remember? At first I was coming along to keep you company. By the end of the trip, I had written a new definition for a travel companion—in our case, it included being a bag packer, bag lugger, bed board carrier, cushion finder, and anything else that needed doing!

The mood of the whole trip was dampened because of your injury, but I learned a lot about being a practical help. I realized that there were little things I could do for you that would help to make things easier. Then there were big things, too. Some of the meetings we took on weeknights were way out in the bush. It took quite a few hours to reach those outback towns by car. Your back would never have made it. Luckily, I was able to fill in for you. I became very accustomed to taking care of you. When we arrived at a new place, I talked to the women in charge about what you could and couldn't do, what sort of chair you had to sit in, when and where you would counsel people, and anything else that came up. Then, about halfway through the trip you started to feel better. You no longer needed me to do all the little practical things I had become used to doing. All of a sudden, I felt unnecessary. I had to realize that you still needed me, but in a different capacity.

It was your practical love that helped me lean on your moral support when I felt better. Having seen you in action doing tough jobs for me, I didn't need to prove your heart concern. I knew I could bank on it. That was a marvelous time for us, Judy. I'll never forget it. God brought us together in a totally new way—as adults serving Jesus—as a team.

Love lugs luggage
stays up late on the phone
making endless arrangements,
smiles at strangers
and even makes friends out of grumpy
taxi drivers!

Love washes clothes in little hotel basins
gives up the best mattress
and walks hot streets finding cool drinks
for tired throats.

Love that is love
has muscles—
they are grown—
doing love!

Love washes blouses at midnight
leaves meals ready in the fridge
with little notes and endless instructions
fastened on with sticky tape.
Love picks you up at school as a surprise
When you could just as easily
take the bus,
Just for a chance to see you smile.
Love never counts the miles walked
so never notices the extra one,
love laughs
and cries,
love lives and
tries.

Love persists like a disciplined athlete
determined to win the crown
for costly caring
Love that is love
has muscles,
they are grown—
doing love!

Talk Time

1. What qualities are important to look for in your Boaz? Discuss.

2. Read 1 Corinthians 7:26–35. What are the advantages of the single state? Do you agree with Paul?

3. How does time enhance relationships?

4. Think of one practical thing that your mom/daughter has done for you. Thank each other.

5. Discuss some ways to give each other gifts of time, not things.

Love Remains

CHAPTER FIVE

Divine love is independent, says C. S. Lewis. It needs nothing to feed its power or worth. It pours out its care on the dependent one. Divine love is gift love. Then there is need love. The dictionary defines need love, or dependent love, as "being determined, influenced, or controlled by something else."[1] All relationships incorporate some element of dependence.[2]

Ruth, for example, was dependent on Naomi when the two first arrived in Bethlehem. Ruth didn't know the people or their customs, and so she had to rely on Naomi to introduce her to that new way of life. Later on in the story, Ruth depended on Boaz too. Her survival was determined by the food she obtained while gleaning in the fields, and so it's easy to see how Ruth was influenced by the amount of barley Boaz provided for her.

Don't you think dependence has a lot of advantages for everyone involved?

Of course. The depender finds comfort and security in this type of relationship because someone is always there to lean on. Many years ago when we were on one of our Holy Land tours, I realized how much I was influ-

enced by what Dad said to me. It was a day when we were sailing very slowly on our Greek ship. Dad asked the captain if we could move a little faster, and the captain replied that the boat already was going as fast as it possibly could. So we spent our time staring intently into the ink blue Mediterranean looking for dolphins. All of a sudden there was a huge splash. I ran to tell Dad that we thought we'd seen the fish. When he saw the next splash, he knew immediately that it wasn't caused by dolphins— we were being shelled! Shells landed on each side of the ship before the crew had a chance to sprint to the back of the boat and raise the Greek flag. I was scared and asked Dad if we would be hit. He confidently said, "No, if they'd wanted to hit us, they would have done so by now. They're just warning us to move further out to sea!" Without hesitation, I believed him.

The funniest part of that story was the way the ship took off out to sea at a terrific rate despite the captain's earlier assurance that it couldn't possibly sail one knot faster!

That was hysterical! It wasn't surprising to see that our ship and the shelling made the front page of many newspapers the next morning. We learned that the day before the bombing, some Israelis had snuck into Lebanon behind a tourist ship and murdered four colonels. So when we were seen moving slowly along the Lebanese coast, with no identifying flag flying, the tense, suspicious soldiers fired to warn us we were sailing too close to their territory.

It was like something out of a movie. You don't expect things like that to happen.

That's true, but it was exciting.

When Pete was a little boy, he climbed up onto the top of a wall and shrieked out, "Daddy, Daddy, come and catch me. I'm going to jump." Dad smiled and opened up his big, safe father's arms to Pete. "Go ahead," he said, "jump!" Pete leaped through the air with gay abandon, sure that his father would do whatever was necessary.

About the same time, Pete was also learning how to swim—or more correctly—was learning how to dive before he learned to swim! He made sure Dad was somewhere in the vicinity and then took to hurling himself into the deep end in various shapes and splashes. Dad had to pull him out and shake the water out of him many times! Now that was foolhardy, and he was reprimanded severely for it, but I couldn't help thinking what a marvelous example this was of total trust in his father. Peter never doubted his dad would be there to rescue him. He counted on his presence. Love counts on the presence of the one who has promised to return his love. It's a marvelous thing in this day and age to be able to count on someone's word, to trust a person's statement of intent, to know it's safe to depend. Children need someone to depend on. It gives them a great bedrock of stability. Then, over time, the depender feels secure enough to gain confidence in himself and branch out on his own.

When I went away to college, I learned to branch out on my own. For my first eighteen years, you and Dad had influenced my life, and within our home, I felt comfortable and secure. Then when it came time for me to make my own decisions, I had enough confidence to do it.

For example, Wheaton gave me many opportunities to think for myself. I was asked questions about my theological beliefs concerning the woman's role in the church that couldn't be answered with just yes or no. I had to explain why I believed certain things. The security you'd given me in my growing years helped me to trust my own ideas and beliefs and stand up for what I thought was right.

Curiously enough, children's dependence gives parents a sense of security, too. They feel worthwhile and useful. There's nothing quite so warm as a feeling of being necessary. When Dad traveled for weeks—and sometimes even months—on end during the early part of our marriage, I had the double responsibility of being Dad and Mom while he was away.

The burden was a heavy one though it was shared by the loving community who worked with us. It gave me a great sense of self worth. When you fell off a donkey the day after Dad left for a three-month tour of ministry, when Dave failed an important school entrance exam and needed extra schooling, and when you all got measles one after another, there was no way I could feel unnecessary. I loved it all—not the measles or the failed exam or the broken arm—but the self-confidence it lent me. I coped, and this made me aware of qualities I didn't know I possessed. Mothering brings a marvelous sense of destiny—an inner recognition that tells you God has made you for a purpose and in that lies value.

The need to be needed is quite legitimate. As Lewis reminds us,

... we must be cautious about calling need love 'mere selfishness.' No doubt need love like all our impulses, can be selfishly indulged—a tyrannous and gluttonous demand for affection can be a horrible thing. But in ordinary life no one calls a child selfish because it turns for comfort to its mother—nor an adult who turns to his fellow for 'company'—since we do in reality need one another ("it is not good for man to be alone").[3]

The problem comes when our need love ceases to be governed by a gift love—as Lewis succinctly puts it—when "God is not God of our loves."[4] Then need love can bring death to a relationship instead of bringing life.

Explain that in terms of adult friendship.

The best personal illustration I can give is one I have used many times before and always with good effect. That's probably because I speak to so many middle-aged women like me who are struggling with the empty-nest syndrome.

I know what you're going to share—about Dave and Jenny.

Right. Dave and Jenny. I'll never forget Dave's arriving home from college with two unexpected things—a beard and a girlfriend! I welcomed them both into the house. What else could I do? "I hope you don't mind, Mom," Dave said, "but Jenny's come to stay for ten days." "I don't mind at all, dear," I replied with a tight smile. Dave didn't seem to see the tight smile—or anything else but Jenny for the next ten days. It was awful! I rose early to pour his favorite cornflakes into his favorite breakfast dish, only to be beaten to the draw by my rival! "Never mind," I comforted myself. "There's still his wash!" Why is it I always wanted to do your wash when you kids came home? I never wanted to do it while you were living here!

Because you needed to be needed?

I guess so! Anyway, it was a lost cause. By the time I managed to get the question out, I was met by David's cool answer, "You don't need to bother yourself, Mom. Jenny's taken care of it." In my washing machine mind you—all tumbling around with hers. That was the last straw.

I remember you exploding about an egg or something.

The first thing Dave asked me to do for him that week was to cook him an egg. I never thought I'd be so excited about a hen and its produce! I began the exercise only to be told by my son, "Not that way, Mom. Jenny will do it!" That was it! I stormed into my bedroom to fall on my face on my bed in floods of tears.

Dad told Dave to follow you, and Pete and I looked at each other in awe. We'd never seen you so upset!

Poor Dave! He appeared in the room like a puzzled elf and said, "Mom—over an egg???"

"It's not the egg, Dave," I replied stiffly, "It's what the egg represents!"

"Well, Mom," replied Dave ever so patiently, "What does the egg represent?" It was only then I was able to tell him because it was only then I fully realized it myself. I needed to be needed, and Dave didn't need me anymore! We prayed about it together.

I very nearly destroyed the very thing I was trying to keep—my relationship with Dave. Need love needed to submit to God's love—to His authority and control. Then it would let go—and paradoxically find itself given back again.

You're in good company, Mom. As Erich Fromm, the famous psychologist says, "The mother-child relationship is paradoxical and in a sense, tragic. It requires the most intense love on the mother's side, yet this very love must help the child grow away from the mother and to become fully independent."5

How did you cope, Mom, with not being needed by us kids anymore?

For me it wasn't particularly difficult. You kids and Dad had already helped me to develop my own gifts and abilities. When you were still in junior high and high school, I realized that you had to be given more independence. Suddenly, I had a lot of time on my hands and started to use it to minister to women. As you grew older and needed me less and less, I had more and more time for the ministry. So, in a sense, I coped by coming to the realization that even if you kids didn't need me anymore, there were lots of other people who did.

I used to hear my friends who were a little bit older than I talk with dread about the empty-nest syndrome. I could never understand it. In fact, I can't grasp the problem now. For a Christian who understands the hurting heart of our world, there is no reason for the nest ever to be empty. Our nest has been full of birds with broken wings since you all flew away to your own green glades! Then, too, I've kept a little corner for the "grand eggs"!

Mother! But that's an excellent point. Too many mothers feel that they are useless once their children leave home. Instead, they should be spending that time helping others. So many charities could use volunteers.

Or what about churches?

That's another possibility. If people would just read the church bulletin, they'd realize how much they are needed.

Another idea is to go back to work or school. Take a chance and try to fulfill your dreams. Now is the time to do it.

Too many times mothers fall apart physically, emotionally, and spiritually during this period. Some turn to alcohol or drugs or soap operas while others decide to sleep away the loneliness. Those aren't answers to the situation.

I don't suppose Naomi turned to alcohol when Ruth began to gain her independence.

Ruth was dependent on Naomi for a while, but then she found a job and became the breadwinner of the family. When this happened, Naomi became dependent on Ruth for survival. "Then she took it up and went into the city, and her mother-in-law saw what she had gleaned. So she brought out and gave to her what she had kept back after she had been satisfied" (Ruth 2:18, NKJV).

It is interesting to see that even though Ruth became independent, she didn't abandon her mother-in-law and try to make it on her own. She didn't use the opportunity to walk away from the relationship. Instead, she realized the way Naomi had cared for her when she had been the depender and tried to repay Naomi for her kindness. She shared her earnings with her mother-in-law. In other words, she was willing to give Naomi the things that defined her freedom.

Unfortunately, during adolescence most mothers and daughters don't act in the way modeled by Naomi and Ruth. I know in our relationship it was a lot easier to use any tiny bit of independence as an opportunity to walk away from the relationship. For example, do you remember when I waitressed during my senior year? The money provided by the job helped to give me more independence. I could buy things without always having to ask you first. A couple of times I wanted to buy some new fashion and you said that I didn't really need any more clothes. I retorted, "Well, I'll buy it with my own money if you won't get it for me." I was using this independence to go my own way.

Learning how to handle independence correctly has to be one of the biggest hassles of adolescence.

It isn't the only problem though. The time when many children reach adolescence is also the time when many parents reach midlife crisis.

In other words, when Mother is at her worst so are her kids!

During this period, parents are realizing that a lot of their life has already passed. They figure that they have another twenty years or so left to work, so they begin to question their job and their lifestyle. "Am I doing what I really enjoy doing?" "Have I accomplished anything important during my life so far?" or "Is there anything I really want to do before it is too late?" Until this point, the focus has been on their kids, so parents begin to grasp onto their children to try to discover their own identity. Nothing is wrong with this, except that it usually occurs when kids reach adolescence and want their independence.

So what happens?

If you're not careful, you can end up having a huge tug-of-war that finishes with a broken relationship.

But if this is all part of normal development for everyone, how do we avoid the alienation?

Both parties have to realize what is happening. Teenagers and parents need to be patient with each other. Obviously there will be some fights, but the chasms that are formed can be bridged through time.

That was true for us, Judy. We had our battles, but we were able to call a truce. In those days our biggest arguments were over clothes and friends.

You always wanted to pick out my clothes for me, but your English taste made it hard for you to understand American fashion. In England, you all wore school uniforms, but over here we didn't. For a while you had a hard time allowing me to wear blue jeans to school, because you were used to children having to dress up. But after fighting about the issue, we finally compromised. Most of my friends wore blue jeans every day, so we decided that I could wear them once a week.

I'd almost forgotten about that.

Do you remember when we were still meeting at the old church? On Sunday evenings the building couldn't hold all of the people coming to the services, and so the kids usually ended up sitting on the floor at the front of the sanctuary. One Sunday morning, Dad announced the program for the evening service and added as an afterthought that all the young people should dress very casually because they would be sitting on the floor as usual. We were so excited. Dad had actually said that we could wear blue jeans to church. The only problem was that you hadn't heard Dad's announcement, so when we barged into the kitchen to tell you, you almost had a fit.

I was so shocked. In England, everyone always dresses up for church.

I couldn't imagine going in jeans. I waited till Dad and I were out of earshot (we had agreed years ago to argue our way to agreement in private) and asked him what on earth he was doing. "Jill," he replied, "isn't it more important that the kids want to go to church than what they wear to worship? If you're not careful, you'll cause a rebellion over a bit of cloth."

And we did get to wear jeans.

Yes you did—clean, new blue jeans, not old, ratty ones.

Not only did you try to choose my clothes, but you tried to pick my friends for me as well.

Judy, you have to see this from a mother's perspective. Until then, you had turned to me with your joys, struggles, victories, and defeats. When you reached thirteen, all of this changed. I wasn't the primary influence in your life anymore, your friends were.

That can be a real problem, can't it? If you get in with the wrong crowd, they can influence the rest of your life. I remember starting to hang around the wrong sort of people when I was thirteen. I wasn't interested in the church youth group because I had more fun doing other things.

I think I tried to manipulate and control you to such a degree that I pushed you further away from me. It never worked, but it's a common mistake. I began to play God. God is omniscient—all knowing—so I became inquisitive, bugging you with incessant questions such as "Who was that on the phone?" or "Where are you going tonight?" or "Whose handwriting was that on the letter that came this morning?"

God is omnipotent, so you began the power play, trying to control me. Until my senior year in high school, you had determined my involvement in the church youth group. I went to Sunday school, Bible studies, musical rehearsals, and Saturday outings. Then our youth pastor left, and I started to work. I didn't have the time to attend all of those functions and had to select just one. Now I was in control of that area of my life. You didn't like that!

And God is omnipresent! That was the killer—trying to be everywhere at once in case I missed something. I fell into bed at night exhausted. But, then, that's what happens when you try to play God. You don't have what it takes! It was a huge relief to let God be God and start to be me again.

Of course, I had no idea you were going through all of that. I thought you were playing games with me. There was one girl I hated. You loved her and decided you wanted us to be friends. Every time I got home from school, you would meet me with a bright, "Hi, Judy, guess who's coming over?" I didn't need to guess!

It didn't work, did it? And yet it gave me a clue. If I could surround you with the right sort of peer group to pick from, and use our home for the meeting ground, then you would have the opportunity to pick the right friends for yourself.

I liked that. I knew our house was a place I could always bring my friends.

That was the adjustment I had to make—to let you bring your friends home, not to pick one special one out for you. Your friends were not all believers, but we tried to win them to the Lord.

Dad told me not to go to school and be intimidated by my friends who weren't Christians but rather to look at the whole situation positively. He said, "Stop saying, 'I'm the only one,' and start saying, 'I'm the first one.'"

Most people think of peer pressure as a negative thing. It helped me as a parent to realize that peer pressure has a positive side to it. Dad helped me, as well as you, to see the influence we could have together on your group of friends.

When Dave and Pete began sports, you used to provide soft drinks and cookies as an alternative to the beer parties.

And when end-of-year celebrations began at school, the church put on an all-night lock-in at the YMCA.

Lots of my friends came to that. I don't think they really wanted to be part of all the other things that were going on, but there wasn't a viable alternative.

It's up to parents and the church to provide that option.

It isn't just kids who are intimidated by peer pressure. Adults feel it too. That's why they may try to achieve their social ambitions through their children.

They can be so intent on their children being popular at all costs that the child finishes up paying the price. In other words, parents can be fulfilling their own social ambitions through their children. Perhaps Mom isn't as popular at the club or in the neighborhood as she secretly wishes to be. Her opportunity can come vicariously as she encourages her son or daughter who seems to have an in with the "in" crowd—and this despite the fact that the "in" crowd is rumored to be enjoying doubtful pursuits in doubtful places. A parent can say, in effect, "Accept anyone as a friend if it will mean being popular." Which of us doesn't want our children to be invited to the big house with the swimming pool along with the neighbor's kids? What's more, the problem is exacerbated because we don't want to upset our children, and there is no doubt about it, they will most definitely be upset if everyone else is invited except them. Add this parental pressure to the church's expectations for the Christian parent and you have a struggle on three fronts: the social front; the spiritual front; and the selfish front! Meanwhile, the child is feeling as intensely about it all as the parent.

Friends mean so much to the teen—too much perhaps—but there is nothing a teenager can do about that as long as she or he is at that age. But I never realized adults feel the same way about their friends.

Peer pressure we call it, and pressure it is.

Friends of both parents and child can become a hot-potato issue.

Another complication has arisen in these last few years to add yet more confusion to the child's mind. With the breakup of families, many weekends are spent in two "homes," at two different locations, necessitating making two different sets of friends. If one set of parents has one philosophy concerning the child's friends and the other a contrary one, you can imagine how complicated it all becomes.

That must be tough. I had enough struggles with one set of parents and peers!

A thirteen-year-old told me just the other day, "When I'm with my mom, I'm not allowed to smoke, my mom doesn't drink, and we go to church on Sundays. Then every other weekend I go to my dad's and his girlfriend's. They smoke, offer me a sip of their drinks, and never go to church. It's confusing, especially when I find myself liking the lazy Sunday mornings in bed better than the early mornings in church. At home I have my friends who don't smoke or drink and always go to church on Sundays. At my dad's it's different! What's more, I find myself behaving in two different ways—as if I'm two totally separate people! I don't like it. I don't know who I am anymore!"

No matter how complicated the situation becomes, and how confused the child is, the Christian parents' responsibility is to take the child from dependence to independence. This includes teaching the child a Christ-based set of values that will enable her to make moral decisions for herself.

That means Jesus Christ needs to become more important than parents or peers and our dependence on Jesus helps us not to become self-centered.

When Jesus is first, He helps us not to become self-centered. When Jesus is first, He helps us to know what's next. It may be years of dependence or time for independence or learning interdependence, but whatever season of our lives we face, our relationship with Him gives us the key. His Spirit spreads His love around in our lives and teaches us to want the very best for those who are close to us.

Love grows healthy
children,
Tall and upright like
fir trees
pointing lip to heaven.
Love works hard to
help a child
find love's perfect
plan for its life.
Love lets go,
knowing that's
the only way a
loved one will want to
come home again—
—his own person!

Talk Time

1. Share one way in which you both depend upon each other.

2. *Mother:* Name one fear you have about the empty-nest syndrome.
   Daughter: Name one fear you have about leaving the nest.

3. What do each of you look for in a friend? How important are your friends to you? Discuss.

4. What do you discover about friendship from these verses?

   Example: Proverbs 27:10—Old friends are to be cherished.

   John 11:16   Proverbs 27:17
   John 15:15   1 Samuel 18:1

5. Each give an example of your own struggle with peer pressure.

Love Lets Go

CHAPTER SIX

By the time the story reaches chapter 3, Naomi has realized that Boaz and Ruth have fallen in love. You would think she would be delighted to hear this news, but in her country, there was a law called the kinsman-redeemer principle. It stated that if a wife's husband died, the husband's nearest kin would marry the widow. If the widow had no children, her first child from the new marriage would receive her dead husband's name, and so carry on his lineage.

How did this affect Boaz and Ruth?

Boaz was a near kinsman, and so according to the principle, Naomi could marry him.

Now that was a problem. Boaz and Ruth were in love, not Boaz and Naomi.

Isn't it interesting to see how Naomi coped with this? She decided to relinquish Boaz and gave him Ruth. She accomplished this by asking Ruth a few searching questions to make sure her daughter-in-law loved Boaz, and then she unveiled her plan.

According to Naomi, Boaz was going to be working late, winnowing barley. Ruth was instructed to take her time to get ready and then go down to the threshing floor. Once she arrived, she was supposed to stay hidden until he had finished eating and laid down to sleep.

That was wise advice. We know what our men are like before they've eaten, don't we?

We sure do! Then Ruth was to uncover his feet. This was a symbol in those days of claiming someone for marriage.

So Ruth went and carried out Naomi's plan.

When Boaz realized that someone had claimed him for marriage, he sat bolt upright and asked who was there. Ruth replied that it was she.

Can you imagine the relief that Boaz must have felt when he heard Ruth's voice? What a mess it would have been if another maiden had uncovered his feet!

Mom, you're such a pessimist! Boaz knew that Naomi had sent Ruth to him. This whole plan was Naomi's way of saying that she had set aside her claim.

"The Lord bless you, my daughter," he replied. *"This kindness is greater than that which you showed earlier: You have not run after the younger men, whether rich or poor. And now, my daughter, don't be afraid. I will do for you all you ask. All my fellow townsmen know that you are a woman of noble character"* (Ruth 3:10-11).

Boaz was thrilled and demonstrated how he felt with compliments.

He commended Ruth for her kindness to her mother-in-law. He, like everyone else, realized how difficult a relationship this had been.

Then he thanked her for choosing him rather than another man. I think Ruth was a very beautiful young woman and therefore could have had any man she wanted.

Finally, Boaz paid her his highest compliment. He said that all the townspeople knew that she was a virtuous woman.

We have to remember that Ruth was the Moabitess. She was a foreigner. But she had displayed such a beautiful example in all her relationships that now everyone agreed; she was a Proverbs 31 woman!

How romantic! Everything turned out so perfectly for them. When you stop to think about it, Naomi was a remarkable woman. If she hadn't relinquished Boaz, then none of that could have taken place.

Oh, yes. If Naomi had been possessive, everything would have turned out differently. She would have ruined at least three relationships.

That happens so frequently. Many parents don't know how to relinquish their kids, so they end up destroying the very thing they're trying to keep.

When a baby robin reaches a certain age, its mother pushes it out of the nest. I can imagine the baby bird feeling very badly about that and the mother feeling even worse—but it has to be done. Letting go, or insisting that the dependent one lets go, begins very early in life! We call it relinquishment. The process begins the day the little one is born. As the late Princess Grace of Monaco once observed, "With the first pangs of birth, one begins to say farewell to one's child. For no sooner has it entered the world than others begin to demand their share. With the baby at one's breast, one keeps the warmth of possession a little longer!"[1] One is reminded again as soon as the child is old enough to go to school.

Didn't you teach kindergarten when you were newly married?

Yes, I did, and I can still remember the poor mothers bringing their children along to school for the very first time. It was awful. I taught in Liverpool, and the classes were very large. Imagine having fifty four- and five-year-olds all starting school on the same day! The parents would bring their little ones to the door of the classroom and then run around the corner of the building until they reached the window. They would hammer on the glass or wave furiously to attract their offspring's attention. Of course, as soon as the little things saw their mothers, their stiff upper lips dissolved in quivering cries of distress. It was catching like measles, and I was left with a roomful of wailing wet kids! I can tell you it didn't take me long to make some curtains for that window!

It's harder for the mothers than the children. The kids settled down as soon as the parents were out of sight, didn't they?

Of course they did—even before the parents were out of the playground! I used to feel really sorry for the moms; although parents have to be reminded of the fact that relinquishment begins as soon as the child is born.

Could we define relinquishment as surrendering the need to be needed?

Yes, I think that's good. Webster's dictionary says relinquishment is "renouncing or surrendering something owned, as a plan or policy."

If parents know they have to let go, why is it always so hard?

A mother finds it difficult for many reasons. If only she can believe she's doing the best possible thing for her child, she will find it easier. Fear was the biggest bear for me. I loved you so much that I felt I couldn't afford for you to make any mistakes. Even one was far too dangerous to allow. Of course, while you were in grade school it was a little different, even though my fertile imagination had you abducted by strangers, dying of cancer, or maimed in a sports accident!

Mom! I can't believe you thought of all those things!

Those things are enough to cause a mother to lock up her child in a plastic bubble—to isolate her from the world's germs forever.

But don't you protect your child by exposing her to some germs so that she can produce her own defense mechanism?

Right. Therein lies the delicate balance. How many germs are too many? That's the dilemma. When is the child healthy and mature enough to be exposed to such a hostile environment?

That's a good point. Relinquishment is a necessary risk parents have to take.

How can moms and dads cope with all their fears when they carry them alone? I was reading Psalm 43 this morning. The writer was relating why he was fearful. He went to God's altar and praised Him even in the midst of his fears. I love the last verse when he starts to ask his soul questions.

He indulged in some soul searching, you mean?

Right! "Why are thou cast down, O my soul? and why art thou disquieted within me? hope in God: for I shall yet praise him, who is the health of my countenance, and my God" (Psalm 43:5, KJV).

There are real reasons to be disquieted within when you look without. But if you are constantly going to God for an inner confidence (which is what "hope" means), a happy, healthy attitude can be the result.

In fact, that's where relinquishment starts, isn't it? Facing reality with God; knowing the thing has to be done, the risk has to be taken. It begins on your knees.

Yes, Judy, it does. It's God who helps us face up to reality, because He is the God of reality, For instance, there is the reality of growing old. God helps us face up to that. I was getting my passport renewed the other day, and there was a quip written above the passport window in the shop that said, "If you really look like your passport photo, you're not fit enough to travel!"

We can giggle at our wrinkles and graying locks, but in the end we need a heavenly perspective on the aging process. God gives us that healthy outlook. We can know we were born on time, are growing at the right rate, and will be dead on time, too! I know the Lord has helped me accept the changing times and seasons and along with that has enabled me to accept the reality of relinquishment. That doesn't mean finality isn't frightening. There is a finality in babies changing into children and children into teenagers and teens into adults. It's a strange anomaly that change is final!

The older you get the harder it is to change.

Absolutely—habits die hard. It makes a lot of sense to have your family when you are young enough to adjust easily.

And yet the largest adjustments are called for when you get older.

When we came to the States, for example, I was thirty-five. That was young in a way, but I'm pretty sure if we had immigrated when I was twenty-five, it would have been easier. On the other hand, you kids had no problems at all adjusting. I felt I was on vacation, but you children settled right on in and took to your new environment like ducks take to water.

Do you have an example of that?

Sure. Our accents! Actually, I think the Americans have the accent and we speak English—but anyway, Dad and I have kept our English brogue a lot longer than you have. In fact, when we first arrived, I recollect members of the church hiding behind pillars or sneaking up on the three of you when you were lost in conversation to hear you speak "English." It took all of three or four weeks before Pete appeared totally Americanized, language and all! I had to learn to relinquish your lovely English accents and be glad that you had adjusted to the move so naturally! Of course, that was just the beginning of an ongoing process.

Parents don't just wake up one morning and say, "Today we're going to relinquish our eldest son." The poor boy wouldn't know what had hit him! As you said earlier, Mom, this process begins the day your child is born.

Parents relinquish their babies to nurses in the hospital right after they're born; their toddlers to babysitters; their four- and five-year-olds to preschool teachers; their adolescents to friends of the same and opposite sex; and finally, their young adults to that one special person.

Each time we do it, it becomes a little easier.

It does?

Well ... maybe it seems easier because we've already done it a few times. You know the saying, practice makes perfect.

Whenever I think of this whole process I remember Hannah. She couldn't have children, so she went to the temple and made a vow to the Lord. If God would give her a son, then she would lend this child to Him. God answered her prayer and Hannah had a son called Samuel. She kept him for about three years and then took him to the temple to keep her word.

That's real relinquishment! In a sense, all parents should act like Hannah. All our children are gifts from God. We need to give our kids back to the Lord so that they can learn to serve Him and fulfill His purposes for their lives.

Poor Hannah; she had wanted a baby for so many years. Yet once she finally had a child, he was hers for only such a short time. Can you imagine the struggle in that young mom's heart as she prepared her son for the temple?

I can remember when you were three. At that time I was learning to let you go bit by bit. For example, I'd take you to one of your friend's houses for an hour or so to play, then, the next week, you'd go for three or four hours. It's hard to imagine what Hannah must have gone through.

In the back of her mind, she must have known that day was coming.

The crisis comes sooner for some parents and later for others.

That's true. Parents have to know each child thoroughly, because each is so unique and will react differently to freedom.

I know Peter got away with so many more things than Dave or I. Was that because he was more mature than we were?

I don't think that was exactly the case. Pete was number three. We practiced on you two, and then were able to modify our rules for Pete.

I agree with what you're saying, Jude. It's such a hard job. With each decision, doubts come popping into our minds as to whether we have done the right thing.

You must question whether you're letting go too soon or holding on too long.

I've counseled a lot of young adults who are so unsure of themselves. I believe part of this insecurity developed from being given too much freedom too soon.

I read a true story about a teenager who didn't have any rules or responsibilities. She could come and go as she pleased. When I first read the description of that girl's life, I was jealous. But, as her story continued and her world started to fall apart around her, I felt sorry for her. She hadn't been given any guidelines on how she should live her life, and so she had copied those around her. Our world is in such a mess that it was obvious she would get into trouble sooner or later.

On the other hand, overprotectiveness can cause insecurity too. When we were in Australia, I talked to a young adult who was very insecure. She explained to me that since she had started college, her parents had given her complete freedom. Although she still lived at home, she didn't have to abide by any rules.

That sounds pretty normal to me. When you turned eighteen and went away to school, you had complete freedom.

True, but there was one major difference. This girl's parents hadn't been gradually relinquishing her. Until her eighteenth birthday, she'd had some very strict rules. All of a sudden, she had no guidelines.

She wasn't prepared for the change.

She hadn't had time to readjust her thoughts and lifestyle. In a sense, her parents had thought and acted for her for eighteen years and then all of a sudden she was dumped out on her own. That's scary.

Do you think it helped when we gave you curfews that gradually diminished as you grew older?

Yes. Later on, when I didn't have a curfew, I knew what times to use as boundaries. You gave me a framework that I could use when making my own decisions. It's almost like writing a book. When I was very young, you had to write everything for me. As I grew older, you could ask me for input about the storyline. Pretty soon, all you needed to write was the outline. Now we're writing a book together!

Naomi and Ruth wrote their own love story together too. Naomi didn't just dump Ruth out on her own all of a sudden either. Trust had been grown little by little, and Naomi was careful to give Ruth a framework to work from. Ruth trusted Naomi enough to promise "All that you say to me I will do" (Ruth 3:5, NKJV), and Naomi trusted Ruth out of her sight.

I struggled with trusting other people. I always felt you were trustworthy, but was Boaz? What about the people at work, or the neighbors, or your friends? In the end, I learned to trust those you children trusted!

For example, by the time you chose your marriage partners, I had relaxed considerably, I had given you freedom early enough to see you made good choices in your close relationships.

But you didn't always act like you'd relinquished us.

We say we have let people go, and yet it's the little things that show us in no uncertain terms that we still want control. Relinquishment is giving up control, and that's a terribly difficult thing to do!

Even though it was so hard, Greg relinquished you for five long weeks. That was so good of Greg. You'd been married only a little over a year.

Actually, the process began a lot earlier. Do you remember calling me about three months after I'd gotten married?

You know I call you more than once a month. Which time are you talking about?

You wanted to know if I had any suggestions for a travel companion to go to Australia with you. I gave you three or four names and then asked Greg if he had any suggestions. Immediately he said, "What about you?"

That's right. I heard Greg and thought it was a wonderful idea.

The only problem was that I was trying to put Greg through graduate school. But I was open-minded, and so Greg and I began to pray about it. If God wanted me to accompany you to Australia, He would have to give me a new job that was flexible enough to allow me to quit without too many problems. Also it would have to be part-time, because I would be sharing a lot of the meetings with you, and I would need time to prepare and practice my talks. Finally, the part-time job would have to pay as much as my old one.

God answered all of our prayers.

Yes He did. He gave me a part-time job that paid almost as much as my full-time one. Instead of leaving home at 6:45 A.M. to get to downtown Chicago by 8:00 A.M. and arriving home again at 5:00 P.M. , I now worked from 10:30 to 2:30. Also, the job was right across the street from my apartment. God couldn't have given a clearer sign that He wanted me to go to Australia with you.

Greg was so supportive through the changing of jobs and the preparation for the trip.

He felt that his involvement in my ministry was to support me both emotionally and financially.

And he did just that! I thought it was marvelous to see the way Greg relinquished you to me after only fifteen months of marriage.

It seemed quite natural to me. Because Greg and I are both pastors' kids, we have seen relinquishment modeled for us all our lives. I watched you and Dad relinquish each other so that Dad could spend ten months out of every year preaching to people in other countries.

Relinquishment has been a way of life since we first got married. When Dad traveled for the bank for the first two years of our life together, we sort of got used to it. Then, as you say, he traveled for the Lord for the next period, and he's kept going ever since! But I won't say it wasn't hard to let him go. Many Christians said to me, "How can Stuart possibly fulfill the biblical role of a father and go away all the time?" I answered, "How can he possibly fulfill the biblical role of an evangelist and stay at home all the time?" I knew the answers just as I knew without a shadow of a doubt it was the right thing for us to be in the youth mission at that period of our lives. But knowing something is right doesn't always make it an easy thing to do! I used to think about how God must have felt giving Jesus up to live away from his home for thirty-three years. He understood. God is love and love relinquishes.

It must have been hard for Dad, too!

I never realized how hard until I began to travel myself. Most of the time I'm on my own and there are many nights when I'm in a lonely hotel room. I understand in a new way what those ten years of traveling were really like for your dad. At least I had you three kids around me, but he had no one—no one, that is, who "belonged" to him. Of course, people are marvelously kind and considerate most of the time, but when you are born to belong to your wife and kids, there is a hungering for family that is hard to describe in words. Relinquishment means staying hungry while you see to God's work. Love stays hungry, determined to see that the work is done. And you know, Judy, you understand something about that. You gave up your dad, too.

I suppose so. It didn't seem abnormal for me because I knew he was doing God's will. God gave Dad back to me in a special way. There are not too many high school seniors who receive a trip around the world for their graduation present.

You'd better explain that. It sounds very glamorous.

Dad took me to Bangladesh, India, Singapore, Taiwan, Hong Kong, China, and the Philippines. In each of those countries we stayed with missionaries, and Dad had the opportunity to minister to them. Just seeing the gratitude on those people's faces and noticing Dad's joy made me realize why God had picked him for this special ministry.

That was so precious to see you two leave on that trip together. It was the beginning of a beautiful relationship.

I believe God has given you and me a similar closeness because we were both willing to relinquish each other, too. It's funny, when we moved to America, I thought we'd see a lot more of you and Dad. Well, Dad was around a little more because he had a church to minister to, but then you started to travel and speak. For the first ten years of my life, I shared my dad with the world; and for the last years, I've shared you. Other women needed to hear about Jesus more than I needed a mother to be at home twenty-four hours a day. I never minded your going, Mom, because I knew you were doing the right thing. The best part of all of this is that He has given you back to me.

Not many married daughters see their mom as much as you see me! God always has His neat surprises around the corner.

Like writing this book together?

And making sure you and Greg live near a major airport!

That's important because even though we've both let go, we still enjoy whatever time we can spend together. God has really helped me to make this huge adjustment. He has shown me that my earthly relationships will always include letting go of those I love. But He has also shown me that He'll always be there to help me through the process. I never have to let go of Him!

And He never lets go of us! I often wonder if I've been allowed such an unusual experience in life so I can share with others the help I've had from God. It's His constant presence with all of us that links us when we are apart. We may be separated physically, but we're one in spirit. We share a closeness that transcends material distance, that travels the miles to bind us together. Prayer is the place to meet. Jesus grows relationships that are bathed in prayer. What would we do without Him?

Relinquishment doesn't
grab or clutch.
Clutching crushes love
Love can't breathe easily
when it's controlled
by possessive
hands.
Trust grows best
when it's planted in
respect.
It flowers in profusion
when joys are shared.
Letting go is a learned
art—
Jesus is the best
teacher.
I need to be the best pupil.
Love will help me
let go—
if I ask Him to.

Talk Time

1. How did the kinsman-redeemer principle affect Naomi, Boaz, and Ruth? What do you learn about Naomi's character in Ruth 3?

2. Read Philippians 2:5–11.
   a) What did God relinquish?
   b) What did Christ relinquish?
   c) What happened to God and Christ's relationship as a result (v. 9–10)?
   d) What do you learn from this?

3. Make a list of the things you need to relinquish. Pray about them together.

Love Is a Teacher

Relinquishment involves an understanding of the uniqueness of another person. Our children are not supposed to be carbon copies of us. God has made them according to His plan and design.

Dad gave a good illustration of this concept in his sermon on Father's Day. He talked about the way a naval commander is given a packet of sealed orders when he sets off on a wartime exercise. When the ship is out at sea, the commander breaks the seal, opens the packet, and discovers the instructions.

The child, according to the Bible, is formed in its mother's womb with God's purposes in mind. Psalm 139 tells us,

My frame was not hidden from you when I was made in the secret place. When I was woven together in the depths of the earth your eyes saw my unformed body. All the days ordained for me were written in your book before one of them came to be (Psalm 139:15–16).

The privilege of parents is to discover what sealed orders are in that precious packet and to assist the child in fulfilling them. What joy it is to explore all that the little one has been created and redeemed to be! This concept must be kept in mind from the child's earliest years.

So if we can keep a sense of discovery and wonder in those formative years, it will prevent us from adding our own instructions to the sealed orders of God. We need to realize that God has specific individualized plans for each child. Our job, as parents, is to wait upon the Lord to learn of His purposes. While we are praying and watching for the unsealing of the orders, we should be training our children in the ways of the Lord. This means that we give them "the same training He gives us, and we are to give it to our children by His direction, through His power, under His authority, and answerable to Him."[1] In other words, we need to deal with them as God deals with us.

Naomi knew that God had designed behavior patterns for His people. She sought to explain these to Ruth; to instruct her in the customs of Israel. In no way did this stifle Ruth's own personality, but rather gave her an opportunity to develop it in the fullest sense. It affected Ruth's behavior, not her personhood.

For example, there were complicated directions for marriage in that day and age, and in Naomi and Boaz's situation, even more problems had to be solved.

After Ruth returned from the threshing floor, she was told by Naomi to "Wait, my daughter, until you find out what happens. ..." (Ruth 3:18). She was obedient even though she couldn't fully understand the legal complications. Putting her trust in God, she waited for Him to work out the details.

Boaz was a near kinsman of Naomi, but there was another man who was a closer relative than he. This other man, therefore, had the prior claim to

Naomi. The matter had to be settled at the gate of the city, the traditional place of justice. The elders of the city congregated there, and they became the witnesses to the change of claim. Boaz had to discover if this man wanted Naomi, Ruth, and the property. Immediately, the man answered, "Yes." But then Boaz reemphasized the implications of the offer. He would not only get the women but the property, too. "Then Boaz said, 'On the day you buy the field from the hand of Naomi, you must also buy it from Ruth the Moabitess, the wife of the dead, to perpetuate the name of the dead through his inheritance'" (Ruth 4:5, NKJV). This meant the nearer kinsman would have to rewrite his will, causing a multitude of problems between his own children and his "new family." Because he wasn't willing to create such a trauma, he said,

"Then I cannot redeem it because I might endanger my own estate. You redeem it yourself. I cannot do it" (Ruth 4:6).

I don't know if I would have taken the risks Ruth and Boaz did. What would have happened if the other man had claimed Ruth in marriage? Boaz and Ruth would have lost each other, and the story would not have had a happy ending. But Boaz wanted to do the right thing, and Ruth didn't take things into her own hands. Instead, she left everything to Boaz. She did what she was told and trusted Jehovah.

How important it is to do things God's way!

That brings us back to training up our children in the nurture and admonition of the Lord.

Nurture, in this sense, means spiritual training by words. We need to explain to the child in his own language exactly what the Lord requires of him. Admonition refers to modeling our teaching. "Do as I do, not just as I say." For example, I can't imagine your sending us to Sunday school, Mom, without coming along. If I had been told to go without you, I don't think I'd have gone for very long.

That was one of our family rules. While you kids were part of the family, you knew you would be in church on the Lord's Day. The subject wasn't up for debate.

A lot of people use the excuse that there isn't a good church or Sunday school to attend.

Jesus never used that excuse. He was always in the synagogue on the Lord's Day.

Since I've moved away from home, it's been hard to find a new fellowship. But because of my upbringing, I realize how important it is to be in church on Sunday.

That's because all your actions are based on the values we've helped you to achieve and accept as your own. The first Sunday school you ever attended was held in our living room at Capernwray. I had started a class for David's little friends because we were without a car, and there was no church close enough to walk to. I dumped your carry cot down in the middle of the floor, about twenty toddlers gathered around it, and we had Sunday school. As far as you were concerned, Sundays were for singing choruses, hearing about Jesus, and coloring Bible pictures. The important part of all that, of course, was that it was fun. You liked it. You didn't grow up with an inbred distaste for church.

People who complain about the lack of programs in their church should begin their own, as you did, right in their own front room.

Or in their own backyard—unless they live in England where there are only two seasons—winter and the second week of August!

Sunday was God's day—that was the principle we tried to build into your every makeup. We were busy every day of the week in His work, but Sunday was special. We tried to make it different enough to set it apart and help you enjoy it.

That didn't mean we always did enjoy it. I can remember being pretty bored in Sunday school sometimes.

That's pretty normal. In fact, I'm always a little suspicious of the child who says he loves going to church. After all, kids are required to sit still for long periods, listen beyond their attention spans, and behave themselves for a whole hour—sometimes more. Their body language often expresses how they feel about it.

I remember Pete sitting in church during his teenage years with his head on his arms. His whole frame was bent into the shape of boredom.

The silent message was not lost on us, or on the watching congregation either. But it was amazing how much of Dad's teaching he absorbed, and that's an important point. Truth can be learned, even by bored kids.

Pete was the only one of us who ever openly rebelled about going to church, wasn't he?

Yes, he was. Fortunately for us, Dave and you were well past that early teenage stage at the time and on your way to being thoroughly active in the youth group. You looked at Pete defying my orders to get himself ready for the evening service and said in amazement, "You mean Dave and I could have rebelled, too?" The thought had never occurred to you for which I was truly grateful!

Pete dug in his heels that night. I wondered what you'd do.

What can you do when your child stands six feet four inches in his stocking feet? All I had left to work with was the respect we had for each other. In the end, he went to church that night because he knew I felt so strongly about it, and he didn't want to hurt me. Children have to know you care about Jesus that much. If they pick up the idea from you that church is boring, they will be encouraged to push you into giving in.

Kids are experts at knowing exactly what their parents are feeling!

When Dad was on the road so much, and I was resenting the mission for asking him to travel, I was trying very hard to hide my struggles from you. I would put you to bed at night and say ever so brightly, "Daddy's away doing things Jesus has asked him to do, isn't that wonderful?"

"No, it's not," you said one night. I couldn't understand why all three of you appeared so irritated and upset until it dawned on me you were picking up my resentment. I used to blame my bad temper on you kids. One day I read a comment that said, "Children don't create your spirit, they reveal it!" That did it. It showed me I had to get my attitude right, and fast. Words, however pretty they sound, can't hide bad attitudes.

But having a good attitude isn't enough. Training also includes giving specific details of rules and expectations.

Right. Where church attendance was concerned, Dad laid it on the line. He let it be known that we would all be in church Sunday morning. Sunday evening was up for discussion if you had a good enough reason to miss it. We also expected you all to involve yourselves in a youth ministry. You had a choice about that. But then again, it wasn't a question of whether you would go, but rather which event you would choose.

You were both pretty adamant about it!

I think many parents are far too lenient about the subject. They may be afraid of turning their children against God by insisting they attend church. I think the adult needs to find the best fellowship possible for the family needs and not keep on going to a particular building simply because their parents laid the foundation. We need to ask ourselves questions such as, "Is it really as boring as the children are telling us? What is the Sunday school program like?" Perhaps we should lend our time, our homes, or use our money to hire a good youth pastor. There are many possibilities open to parents today.

For instance, youth magazines to read, Christian camps to attend, and parachurch youth ministries that are vital and alive.

That's true. Pete was helped by the Fellowship of Christian Athletes more than our own Sunday school program. It really depends on our priorities. If we as parents are more concerned with involving our children in extracurricular school activities than in church ministries, we will have a problem on our hands concerning church attendance!

Your specific guidelines did help us to know exactly what you expected from us. If you had just said, "You have to go to church," we wouldn't have known if that meant once a week or ten times a week.

Don't you think that's one of the biggest problems we encounter while raising kids?

Yes. When I was small, you would tell me to tidy up. I would clean up a little and then continue to play with my toys. You learned to tell me exactly what you wanted. For example, you would say, "Judy, please put all the toys in the living room in the blue box." Or, instead of telling me to get cleaned up, you'd explain that I should take a bath and wash my hair. When I was a teenager, instead of ordering me to come in early from a date, you'd define exactly what early meant.

So many teenagers I've worked with get into trouble for coming in "late." The problem is that their parents have never taken the time to define this word. They consider 12:30 late for a sixteen-year-old, yet the child might define this word as meaning 2:00 A.M. It avoids so many fights if we can be specific with our rules.

I know some girls who've ruined their lives because they didn't understand the rules that were set for them. They were told to "be good girls" when they were out with their boyfriends. According to society, that can be interpreted as doing what everyone else does. Many times, the girls ended up pregnant and without the support of their parents or society.

I was so thankful for the youth leaders during your adolescent years. The "sex talks" they gave once a year were very explicit.

Our youth pastor had three good rules for us when we were out on a date: don't lie down; don't take anything off; and nothing below the neck. Now those were pretty specific, don't you think? And you know what? I never forgot them, and always knew my limits.

The funniest time we ever heard those rules mentioned was at Dave's wedding. Do you remember? Bob couldn't come but he managed to send a telegram that arrived at the reception. It said, "Congratulations—forget the rules!"

Once again, that reminds me of Naomi and Ruth. First of all, Naomi gave her daughter-in-law specific advice. She didn't tell Ruth to go and inform Boaz that she wanted to marry him. Instead, she gave her detailed instructions to follow.

Once Ruth had completed her "assignment," she knew exactly what to do because Naomi had given her boundaries. Naomi told Ruth to sit and wait patiently for Boaz, and Ruth did just that.

When you think about it, parents need to be one step ahead of their kids so they can anticipate any problems along the road of life.

Yet not too far ahead, because if they are, they can place unrealistic expectations on their children.

You mean expecting their seven-year-old to act like a ten-year-old?

That's one example. Unfortunately, many parents push their children too far. Each child reacts differently to the pressure. Some need it in order to work at all whereas others find it too much to bear and decide to opt out on life.

Then there are all those who fall between the two extremes.

For instance, children who believe their parents will love them only if they are at the top of their high school and college classes. Not long ago, I was talking to a smart high school girl about her future. She expressed an interest in attending Harvard as an undergraduate and then going on to Harvard Medical School. She appeared so confident that she would be accepted. I was impressed. But then she went on to describe her family situation. I discovered that her parents had planted this idea in her mind and watered it until it had grown into a full tree. Once again, there's nothing wrong with parents helping their children to reach their full potential, but they have to be so careful that they are assisting in the decision-making process and not making the decision themselves. Dad is so good in this area. When I ask his advice, he always remains neutral, even though he might have a preference. He tries to point out the pros and cons of each option. Sometimes this is frustrating because I want him to tell me what to do.

But he won't do that. He has the ability to let you talk through the decision with him and come to your own conclusions. Sometimes we see you leaning toward choices we ourselves wouldn't make, yet if it's right for you, we have to let you go. I think that Christian parents have high expectations for their children and for themselves, and I think they should have. It's right to want unbelievers to see Christ in us. The problem comes when our hopes are unrealistic. I have not wanted to write about child rearing, simply because I didn't know if I had any right to say anything unless you kids turned out perfectly!

One day Dad asked me if I was waiting until you were all spiritual giants, and I replied, "Yes!"

"Well," he responded, "I don't want my kids to be giants. Giants are freaks! I want my kids to be kids." It was at that point I realized we did have something to say that could be helpful to normal parents—like us—raising normal kids—like you! The conversation also showed me I was expecting unfair things from you. I had to forgive you for being thirteen and approaching spiritual matters as a typical thirteen-year-old. This took the pressure off both of us.

I had to deal with the pressures I'd put on myself, too. I tried so hard to be a super mom and, of course, failed. Then I was so busy feeling guilty I couldn't even be an "unsuper" mom! Dad helped me relax, enabling me to have the freedom to fail.

Sometimes I still don't give myself that freedom to fail. When I was about ten or eleven, I thought that I had to behave "perfectly" because I was a pastor's kid. Obviously I made up a lot of those expectations in my own imagination, but some of this thinking was generated by such statements as, "What would your parents think if they knew about this?" or "Judy, you need to be an example for the other children."

I suppose I got tired of always having to be the example. Now I can look back and consider it from everyone's point of view. Because I was a P.K., there were certain obligations required of me. This was an obvious fact. But I had to also see the positive side. Being a P.K. gave me the opportunity to meet interesting people who invested their time and prayers in my life.

Coming into the pastorate, I was warned by friends to protect you children from unfair expectations. I was led to believe the parishioners would be looking for polite, clean, happy-to-be-in-church kids. P.K.s would never be disobedient, dirty-mouthed, or tell tales. P.K.s would love to hear Daddy's preaching and would always be looking for opportunities to invite their friends to hear it too! P.K.s would be very excited to be introduced to a group of their peers as "the P.K.s" instead of by their real names.

P.K.s would spend all their pocket money on Christian magazines instead of buying fun (but worldly) periodicals such as *People* or *Teen*. P.K.s would dress up when everyone else wore jeans and would be delighted to stick out like sore thumbs. P.K.s would never experiment with drugs and would always be top of their class. The parishioners would say that this was probably because they loved to go to bed really early. Their curfew would be suitably imposed to ensure proper rest and time for devotions. P.K.s would only date the children of elders and deacons and would never be tempted sexually because they were perfectly pure and never thought about their bodies or emotions at all. P.K.s would love to wait every Sunday night until the janitor wanted to lock up, because Daddy was talking to the large lady who was always talking to Daddy! P.K.s wouldn't be able to wait to find out who was coming to dinner or staying overnight so that they could eat leftovers in the kitchen and sleep on the floor so the visitors could have their beds. P.K.s like this, let me tell you, don't exist. And aren't you glad? I certainly am.

I don't know how many of our parishioners honestly believed those things about P.K.s—only a handful I think—but enough to cause a few problems. The vast majority of the church people were wonderful and never laid such heavy loads on you. They were, in fact, fully supportive, understanding, and helpful.

Sometimes expectations are perceived and not actual. "That lady thinks this or that about me," muses the child when "that lady" is thinking no such thing! Perceived expectations can be the hardest things to cope with.

My overreaction to the "P.K." label and rebellion against church activities and Christian friends were my way of saying that I wanted space to breathe and room to grow. To make the mistakes any normal child makes. Luckily you and Dad realized my struggles and shifted your attention away from my church behavior to areas of my life where you could offer positive reinforcement.

At that time, I was doing well in school. You started paying close attention to my report cards and school activities and complimented me wherever possible. But you didn't just look at my academics. You also tried to discover other areas of my life where you could offer encouragement. I wanted to learn how to play racquetball, so you decided that we would play together every Thursday after school. Remember how much fun we had? We started each game with the intent of improving our technique and getting a good workout. But this didn't last very long, because we started to talk. Pretty soon we'd be standing in the middle of the court, relating the events of the day to each other.

That was fine. I was glad for the opportunity to talk with you. Sometimes when we were standing there, you would open up and tell me what you were thinking and feeling. I'm really thankful for racquetball because it gave us a common ground at a time when we didn't have too much in common!

As I grew older, I tried to live up to your hopes for me. The problem was that I thought you expected things that you didn't. We weren't always communicating very well. Because I was obsessed with always wanting to please you, I became too much of a perfectionist. This attitude spread to every area of my life. Exercise became far too important. If I missed a day of running because it was too cold, I couldn't cope. Also, nothing short of my preset distance of three to five miles was acceptable. It didn't matter how much pain I encountered along the way.

Pretty soon I had the same attitude about my studies. Only perfection would be tolerated. One of the big problems was that I was attending Wheaton College, and you can't achieve 100 percent at Wheaton all the time! Then my eating habits began to follow this pattern too. I started counting every single calorie I ate. If I knew that I was going out for dinner on Friday night, I had to suffer on Tuesday, Wednesday, and Thursday so that I wouldn't gain too much weight after Friday's gorge. I rationalized my thinking by quoting 1 Corinthians 6:19 to myself—"Do you not know that your body is the temple of the Holy Spirit, who is in you, whom you have from God? You are not your own; you were bought at a price." If my body was the temple of the Holy Spirit, then I wanted to make sure it was in perfect condition for Him. Therefore, I exercised constantly, studied meticulously, and ate sparingly. I thought my life was in perfect "all around shape."

On top of this, you seemed so proud. You commended me on my disciplined lifestyle. But you also expressed concern about too much self-control. I wanted so badly to please you that all I ever heard were your compliments. Then one day we sat down and had a long talk. I realized that I wasn't driven by everyone else's expectations for me, but by my own perceptions. Together we tried to determine where all of this had begun— do you remember? Through talking with one of Dad's friends and applying some of the lessons I learned in my classes at Wheaton, we began to see the light at the end of the tunnel. I realized my personality had already been formed, and I couldn't change it, so I had to learn to cope with it. For example, I had to realize that I was susceptible to such things as an anorectic mindset because of my type of personality.

A person's drive or ambition can be a useful tool in achieving certain goals in life, but you have to be careful that the expectations you set for yourself or that others make for you don't begin to dominate your lifestyle. It isn't worth it.

Bringing children up in the nurture and admonition of the Lord obviously involves an awful lot more than exposing youngsters to church and being careful not to overload them with unfair expectations, but, then, volumes have been written on this subject. Suffice it to say in the context of this book, that we have taken the things that had the most significance in our own relationship and written about them. The illustrations will be relevant to some. The principles should be applicable to all.

Love works hard to make truth clear
as crystal, easy to understand.
Love believes in Sunday school
in little minds needing little lessons—
about a big God
Love gently instructs those it
loves to accept truth's tenets,
ancient values, moral codes.
Love hopes for a ready response
but makes allowances for
human frailty
Love trusts twice, forgives freely
while expecting the best.
Love is ever patient
using time
to grow a good child;
Replete with the likeness of
its Maker!

Talk Time

1. Read Psalm 139:15–16 together. God has made us all different. As God's sealed orders have been opened, tell what gifts and talents you have discovered in each other.

2. Who do you think should be responsible for the spiritual training of the child? Circle:

   School?   Pastor?   Parent?
   Youth leader?   Self?

3. Do you think children should go to church if they are not Christians? If bored? If teenagers? Give reasons for or against.

4. P.K.s or even children from Christian homes feel a certain amount of pressure to be "super spiritual." Why? What can parent and child do to keep this from becoming a problem?

5. Do you feel that you have unrealistic expectations placed on you? What are they?

CHAPTER EIGHT

Communication: relationships can't survive without it. "Many marriage counselors say that one of the problems in marriage is poor communication,"[1] and it isn't much better between parents and kids. Communication is a two-way street, and unless both parties work at it, the relationship can't grow.

A small boy with an inquiring mind asked his father some questions. "How far is it to the sun, Dad?" "I don't know, son," replied his father. "How many people are there in the world?" "I've no idea," replied Dad. "How do helicopters stay up when the wind drops?" was the next query. "I don't know," answered the older man. "I hope you don't mind me asking you all these questions, Dad," the little boy said uncertainly. At this, the father smiled indulgently and said, "Of course not, son. How are you going to learn if you don't ask questions!"

It's no good questioning Dad unless he learns how to respond. Good communication involves more than just saying, "I don't know"! Of course, the father was communicating something. He was telling his child he knew nothing! This can only frustrate a relationship.

When we come to the subject of relating to one another, we have to give each other a part of ourselves.

This process involves three major stages. The first and most obvious one is talking. This is how we explain ourselves to each other. Every time we speak, we are sharing a part of ourselves with someone else.

That's important to remember because a lot of the words that come out of our mouths are empty or aren't very pretty.

Exactly. What you say tells the truth about who you are. "Out of the abundance of the heart the mouth speaks" (Matthew 12:34b, NKJV).

The second aspect of communication is listening. This involves attending closely to what is being said.

Then the third part of this process must be comprehension.

Whenever two people have a conversation, many obstacles hinder the correct message from getting across. To understand exactly what our friend means, we need to look at what she actually says, how she says it, and what she leaves unsaid.

Let's deal with talking first.

You know, in any conversation there are always three participants: the talker, the listener, and God.

If communication is blocked between any two parties, then the result will be confusion. For example, "In the beginning was the Word [another name for Jesus], and the Word was with God, and the Word was God" (John 1:1). When the Father wanted to communicate with His children, He used a word. He descended to our level and spoke our language. Christ interpreted the Father's wishes to us. The problem was that we didn't want to hear. "He came to His own, and His own did not receive Him. But as many as received Him, to them He gave the right to become children of God, even to those who believe in His name" (John 1:11–12,

NKJV). Those who received God's Word were brought into a close family relationship with the Father. He removed the barrier of sin by His death on the cross. Now Christians can talk with God "face-to-face" as with a friend. As we learn to do this in prayer, we begin to find our relationship with others improves. We need to communicate with God in order to share with others.

It's because I have a personal relationship with Jesus that I even bother to work at communicating at all. Sometimes too many barriers block my efforts and I give up. But when this happens, I quickly realize that Christ wants me to be talking with those I love.

And those we don't love as well!

Sometimes I have a hard time finding the correct words for a given occasion. When the mother of one of my close friends died, I wanted to comfort her. But I couldn't think of the right words to use. Finally I borrowed someone else's and wrote her a short note ending with a beautiful poem I'd read in my devotional book the day before. My friend was very happy that I'd taken the time and effort to encourage her.

I think it's important to try our best to reach out at a time of crisis even when we feel our vocabulary is inadequate. Most people just want to know you care. They aren't concerned with pretty words.

That principle should be used in everyday conversations, too. It's better to communicate something than nothing at all. Silence is dangerous.

Love talks. It refuses to punish by silence. It's the fact that I am a Christian that has made me stop behaving in a juvenile fashion in my own marriage relationship. When we were first married, Dad had a hard time remembering my birthday. Once he forgot because he was hectically busy preparing for a tour of ministry abroad. But I was selfish and piqued and decided I wasn't going to forgive him this time. When he came in from the office that night without flowers in his arms or a present anywhere in sight, I punished him with silence.

"Is anything wrong, dear?" he asked tentatively, picking up my nonverbal message. "No, no, nothing," I replied in that certain way that made sure he knew there was! I was determined to keep him guessing. I was even more irritated by the fact that he didn't keep on guessing! Obviously he had decided to let me get over whatever was bugging me without pursuing the matter. Eventually I told him it was my birthday and he was duly chagrined.

I have learned the lesson of love over the years. I kindly put my birthday in his diary for him. He has many more important things to do in this life than remember my birthday! People are going to hell, and we are called to work together to bring the message of reconciliation to them. I endeavor to make such things as easy as possible for him and not add to the burdens he bears. In fact, last year I forgot *his* birthday. Imagine that!

A lot of people I talk with tell me that they don't have anything in common with their spouses or children and so everyone just does their own thing. In many American homes, everyone eats at different times and then splits in different directions to opposite ends of the house. There's no need to make the effort to debate which TV program we'll all watch because we all have a TV of our own! Our money has made it possible to live in a house full of strangers!

In other words, modern-day materialism really militates against good communication.

When Greg and I were taking the premarital class at church, the leaders strongly advised that we didn't buy a TV for the first year of our marriage. Many young couples spend all their time glued to the box instead of to each other! That's one of the quickest ways to eliminate all forms of communication.

Greg and I have really worked at giving each other our full attention. I am a psychologist and enjoy discovering interesting things about people. Greg, on the other hand, works in real estate. He loves his facts and figures. We have both tried to find areas in each other's lives where we can show interest. This has caused many frustrating conversations, because it means starting from square one and explaining the most basic level of our work to each other. But it's worth it. I want to know what my husband is doing all day long, and luckily, he's interested in my life too!

Another reason I find it really hard to talk things out with people is because I don't want to hurt them by "speaking the truth in love" (Ephesians 4:15). If you level with people without love, you flatten them. Love is the element that helps you to say the hard things without alienating people.

I struggled with my own motherhood in this regard. Nanna used to advise me to "always send your children to bed happy." That was the way we were brought up, but I found there was often a conflict between happiness and holiness. Not that holiness excludes happiness, but naughty children need chastising, if not physically, certainly verbally. Sometimes that meant sending you to bed very unhappy indeed!

I can't believe how perfectly the story of Ruth parallels these principles. Isn't it amazing that so many years ago they encountered the same hurdles we do?

You're referring to the beginning of the story when Naomi said the hard thing to Orpah and Ruth by telling them, "Return home, my daughters. Why would you come with me? Am I going to have any more sons, who could become your husbands?" (Ruth 1:11).

Yes, it must have been difficult for Naomi to say the right thing instead of the selfish thing. Honesty hurts, but, then, love is honest.

If we're going to discuss honesty, look at chapter 1:20–21.

"Don't call me Naomi, … because the Almighty has made my life very bitter. I went away full, but the Lord has brought me back empty."
Honesty implies integrity: "An incorruptible soundness in moral character especially as displayed in fulfilling trusts."[2]

Another definition is a habitual truthfulness.[3]

In other words, you can't practice honesty without respect. You speak the truth because you honor the other person.

Right. I sense a huge respect between Naomi and Ruth, don't you?

Yes. I guess trust comes when you make it clear with words that you expect the other person to behave uprightly.

We need to impart the fact that we trust each other. Do you remember that famous time when I was worrying about your beginning to date and yet we weren't talking about it?

How could I forget! I couldn't understand why you glared at my boyfriends every time I brought them home!

It wasn't that I didn't trust you. I didn't trust them.

How was I to know that? You didn't tell me. All I received from you was very strong nonverbal communication. You didn't say anything.

I'm so glad you took the initiative, or we could have had a cold war. You took me by the hand and marched me into the bedroom, saying firmly, "Mother, I think you and I should have a talk!"

I asked you why you didn't trust me.

And I replied that I did, but I didn't trust your friends! I remember that hurt you because your friends were very special to you and it sounded as though I didn't think much of them.

I know now that it was because you didn't know them very well.

At least we got it out in the open. I was able to let you see I was frightened, and you were able to let me see you were choosing right. You also told me I had to let you make mistakes.

But you said you couldn't afford for me to make any!

Now I realize how silly that was. All of us make mistakes. The problem is that boy/girl mistakes, in this day and age, have such drastic repercussions.

I knew that! We prayed together that all my mistakes would be small ones.

My problem was I didn't trust your judgment. After all, you were only fifteen.

But you can't learn to make good judgments without experience.

The parents' dilemma is knowing when the child is mature enough to handle it. When Dad is talking to parents about this, he uses an excellent illustration. He says being a parent is like being a trampoline. The kid is jumping up and down on the parent, trying to get into orbit, and the parent has to know how tight to keep his trampoline. If it's too tight the child will hit her head on the ceiling, and if it's too loose, she'll break her back on the floor! Then you have the added problem of other kids bouncing up and down at the same time! They all need a different tension.

If you can at least discuss the tension, then you'll have a better understanding of each other's behavior.

Did I stop glaring?

Not all at once!

I'm sorry!

That's OK I did my share of glaring too! I had to help you trust me by proving I was trustworthy.

And I had to honor your choices and pray you through the risks you took in making your own decisions.

Before we're even introduced to Naomi and Ruth, they had obviously learned to speak their minds to each other. In 1:16, Ruth is demonstrating her respect toward Naomi. Basically, she tells her mother-in-law that she will stay with her forever because she loves her.

It's a wonderful thing to be able to tell those who are close to us that we love them. When I was a young teenager, I found it difficult to express how much you and Dad meant to me. So I discovered another way to communicate that very important message. I found cute cards and added my own thoughts and feelings as best I could. Pretty soon, you started writing me little notes, too. I love the way that method of sharing has become a happy habit.

If you can't say it with flare, say it with flowers! You have to start somewhere. If you don't say it, people tend to go and find someone else who will. How many times I have listened to a husband or wife who says sadly, "If only I had learned to express my love, we'd still be together today."

But in the end, using other people's words isn't enough. You have to find out how to say it for yourself.

And that involves a basic knowledge of the English language.

In Ruth and Naomi's situation, there must have been language adjustments. Although their languages were similar, they weren't identical.

Like Spanish and Portuguese?

Yes. When I spent a summer in Ecuador, I realized immediately how important it was to know the exact words for everything. I had been taught the language as it was spoken in Spain, but in Quito, the people had different pronunciations. I learned very quickly to use the South American way of saying things if I wanted to be understood.

So your incentive for learning was to make life easier for yourself and also to make sure you didn't offend anyone?

Yes.

That reminds me of the time I took you three kids back to England for the first time. When we arrived at London airport, we were hot, tired, dusty, and thirsty. Pete, age eight, who had had no problem at all becoming thoroughly Americanized within weeks of arriving in his new country, asked the lady in the restaurant for some root beer. She glared at me and began to tell everyone what she thought of parents who introduced their children to alcohol at such a tender age!

That's right, they don't have root beer in England.

Learning the language of love will necessitate as much care and effort as it takes to master a foreign tongue.

But the incentive has to be there. You've got to want to make life easier for all concerned.

Another incentive to work with words is to be able to bring pleasure to those you love. There's a difference between saying to your husband, "Boy, you're getting fat!" and "I love you when you carry a little more weight. You look so much healthier!"

That's a lot nicer. Compliments are useful. I've been glad of them in bridging broken relationships. If there's a person I'm really struggling to get along with, I try to find something about her that I like and then tell her. Sometimes I haven't wanted to open my mouth and get the words out, but I'm always glad when I've made the effort. I also make myself compliment people who intimidate me. I have a beautiful friend who always dresses meticulously and looks fantastic. When I'm with her, I usually feel insignificant. Sometimes I really like what she's wearing but don't tell her because I figure she already knows she looks great. I have to remind myself that it isn't her fault I'm intimidated and compliment her anyway!

It doesn't really take too much effort to give compliments, to say something kind. I don't mean to be hypocritical or "butter people up," as we say in England. Coming from Britain, I had to learn both to give and accept compliments. It's not a national custom at home. In fact, we tend to tease each other a lot or, as the Americans would interpret it, "put each other down."

Pete was the first one to show me how encouraging it could be to affirm someone with words. He's always been a natural that way. He's been able to mix teasing with compliments. One day he saw me all dressed up for church and said, "Hey Mom, you look like a million dollars." I was thrilled! "Thanks, Pete," I replied. "All green and wrinkled," he shot back! I hit him over the head with a cushion! Love teases only when it's very sure the one who's teased is secure in the knowledge that he's loved!

The same day, Pete found me with my books and Bibles, preparing a message. "I always know where I will find you," he said quietly, giving me a hug. My heart warmed to his compliment. I was encouraged. Affirmation is so important to build another up and not break him or her down. Words can do that.

Look how Boaz used words to affirm Ruth:

"I've been told all about what you have done for your mother-in-law since the death of your husband—how you left your father and mother and your homeland and came to live with a people you did not know before. May the Lord repay you for what you have done. May you be richly rewarded by the Lord, the God of Israel, under whose wings you have come to take refuge" (Ruth 2:11–12).

And listen to Ruth's answer. "You have given me comfort and have spoken kindly to your servant—though I do not have the standing of one of your servant girls" (Ruth 2:13).

When all these habits are practiced over the years, words become like bridges instead of barriers. Learning to talk at shallow levels makes deeper dialogue possible. If we never endeavor to talk about football, we'll never be able to discuss the things that really matter.

Who wants to know about football?

The one who loves the one who loves the crazy sport!

Good communication made my teenage years so much easier. There was the time I wanted to go to that dance during my junior year and stay out all night. When I asked you about it, I also used the opportunity to tell you that I thought a lot of your rules were a little outdated. You didn't totally agree with me, but you were willing to listen to what I had to say. You sat very patiently while I argued my points and then I listened to your side. Between the two of us, we were able to come up with some mutually agreeable guidelines. I could accept those rules because I'd helped to make them. That made the difference! Then you took the time to explain why you were placing such restrictions on me.

But it took time. I remember writing the words "This too will pass" in the front of my Bible to encourage myself. I hated your teenage years to be such a constant battlefield. I was so frightened you would go to college before we had become friends. So it was a great relief when we eventually made it through to happy harmony! Once we arrived at that point, dating began to be fun for both of us.

There were those special occasions—parties and dances—that required shopping together. By that time it was not because we had to but because we wanted to. Or coming in from a date and telling you where we'd been and who we'd been with. I didn't have to tell you, but you had become my close friend!

I can just see Ruth sitting on the edge of Naomi's bedroll and telling her all about Boaz, "He even said to me, 'Stay with my workers until they finish harvesting all my grain'" (Ruth 2:21). And I can just hear Naomi's excited response, "It will be good for you, my daughter, to go with his girls, because in someone else's field you might be harmed" (Ruth 2:22). What a joy, Judy, that our bad times had become bedtimes of blessing before you left home, and a really deep problem surfaced.

I guess it all began that summer at the beach. I hadn't seen Greg or you for eight weeks and was so excited that we had fourteen days to relax together. After everyone retired the first night, Greg and I went for a romantic stroll in the moonlight. Unfortunately, the spell of the evening was broken quite quickly when Greg turned to me and said very seriously that we had to talk. We sat down in the sand and then he began. Over the previous two months, he'd spent his spare time reading books about anorexia nervosa. According to him, I had the same sort of mind-set as the people in those books. I thought he was crazy and told him to drop the subject. The rest of the vacation was full of fighting and loud silences whenever he brought the topic up.

After you returned to school, Greg put you in the car and drove you to Milwaukee, and asked if he could sit down with Dad and me and talk things over. We didn't know Greg very well at the time, but realized what a very special young man we had on our hands! He told us the things he was so deeply concerned about and how he needed our support to help you face the fact that you really had an eating problem. We only had to take one look at you to know he was right. Dad asked you to take him to the airport—he was going out of town—and used that opportunity to ask you to put some poundage on just for him. It was then you realized you couldn't and were able to admit to yourself you had a need. I can't tell you how helpless Dad and I felt. I remember our standing in the kitchen looking at each other after you had left. "Where do we go for help?" I asked. "I don't know," he replied. We were struggling to absorb the immensity of it all. How could our daughter have gotten herself into such a state without our having something to do with it? What had our contribution been? Perhaps we had put unfair expectations on you? Was it the fact that Dad and I were visible models of some sort of achievement and this had intimidated you? Had we not affirmed you as we should? Dad and I had always said to each other, "Judy will never give us any trouble. She wants to please us too much," and suddenly we realized that was the root of the problem. We were not dealing with a prodigal but with a "good child" who didn't believe she was good enough!

I didn't know what to do either. I wanted to put weight on because Dad had asked me to, but I'd developed such a mind-set that I couldn't. Once again, I felt I'd failed you. I talked to Greg about this one night and he asked me what I meant when I said "once again." Through a long discussion, I began to see all sorts of expectations I had thought you had placed on me, which you never had. You or Dad would make a suggestion and I would take it as something I had to do. For example, I entered Wheaton as a biology major. Although I thought I wanted to practice medicine, part of my motivation was that I thought you wanted me to become a doctor. Once I discovered that you only desired for me to be me and do what made me happy, I felt free to make my own decision about my career. After a lot of thought and prayer, I changed to psychology.

It was during one of my classes, when the professor talked about anorexia, that I knew I needed help. I didn't have a serious problem, but I realized that it could become dangerous if I didn't get assistance. After class ended, I approached my teacher and asked if I could talk with him. I told him that I was struggling with my eating habits. He called a friend on the phone and arranged for me to see a young woman who was completing her master's degree with a specialization in eating disorders. Once a week we sat and talked for about an hour. Cara became my sounding board. She was someone set apart from my family and friends and therefore was able to detect things those who were close to me couldn't.

Now I had openly admitted I had a need. I had to live with the people who knew about it for the next two years. Would they think I was strange, I wondered? Being open and honest makes you vulnerable to those around you!

The hardest part of this whole process was after I'd decided to talk with Cara, I knew I had to tell you and Dad what I'd done. I was scared to call because I wasn't sure how you would react.

You'll never know how thrilled we were to get that call! We had been praying so hard that God would send someone to help us. How grateful we were to your friends and to the professors who knew exactly what to do! They gave you a support system. Within a few weeks the initial crisis had passed. The thing had been faced, brought out in the open, and thoroughly talked out, and God had you well on the way back to health.

It was my psychology that showed me what was wrong, and my theology that helped me put it right!

That's a pretty powerful combination, Judy. And that's why you have lots to share when you speak and minister.

I'm finding there are many people like me who feel they do everything they know how to do and it's never enough—people with low self-esteem. I'm able to share the hard lessons I've learned and tell them about the practical help that's available.

I suppose this brings us back full circle.

Right. Once I started communicating with all of you and God about the situation, I started to heal. It's so important to realize that this process always involves God. If we leave Him out, we won't be able to communicate with each other and we'll be in trouble!

When you really trust the Lord, you know He knows all about you but loves you just the same. This lets you accept yourself. Love is like that.

Love never paints an
unfinished sunset,

or makes half a world or a
bird with one wing.

Love always completes the things
He starts.

One day it will all be over and
we will be like Him, but
till then—
Love affirms the loved one
with words
refusing to let silence
punish an offender.

Love isn't afraid to
tell the truth
or face the facts
or level—
but always in love, of course.

Love delights to use ordinary people—
To help people who don't
realize how loved ordinary
people are!

Teachers and friends, boyfriends, fiancés
and even parents
insist we discover we are special;
after all, they tell us,
God thought we were worth
dying for!

Talk Time

1. Which of the three stages of communication do you find hardest?
   Why?
   Talking
   Listening
   Comprehending

2. Read John 1:1–14. Make a list of the initiatives God took. How did
   man respond? What can we learn from this?

3. Name a difficult occasion when you made the effort to communicate
   with someone even though you didn't feel you had the right words
   to say. What was her reaction?

4. Think of one thing you have never been able to talk about honestly
   and openly with each other. If you can, share it now.

5. Give each other a compliment (GO ON!).

Love Listens

CHAPTER NINE

I'm not looking forward to writing this chapter, Judy. Dad says I'm always completing all his sentences for him.

Maybe we'll both learn some necessary lessons and Dad will benefit!

And others too! I know that listening leads to good relationships. It lends itself to happy families and a healthy ministry! What's more, God has called us to listen. Psalm 94:9 tells us, "He ... planted the ear" (KJV). Jesus was always saying that people needed to use their ears. "He who has ears to hear, let him hear," He would say after He had finished His teaching.

You know, in Liverpool the slang word for ears is "lugs." On one occasion I was leading a Bible study with some kids and we came across this verse. One of them with typical Liverpudlian humor said, "Sounds a bit eerie to me!" "Come on now," I remonstrated. "What do you think Jesus meant?" The kids wrestling with the King James language fell silent. Then one replied, "Pin yer lugs back!" I couldn't help feeling that was exactly what Jesus intended to convey. We don't know how to listen and we need to learn.

First we need to learn to listen to Him. God didn't lean out of heaven at Jesus' baptism and say, "This is my beloved Son. Talk His ear off!" He said that He would "let none of his words fall to the ground"! (1 Samuel 3:19, KJV). That gives me the idea that the Father was listening very carefully to His Son.

If earthly fathers would only listen as attentively to their earthly sons! The idea of sacred ears is rooted in the Old Testament.

The priest was given to Israel in order to listen to God, to tell the people what he heard, and then to listen to their response.

Exactly. The New Testament tells us that every Christian is a priest. It talks of the priesthood of all believers (see 1 Peter 2:5, 9).

I like the idea of being able to give my ears to God so He can help me "lend an ear" to people's troubles.

Love doesn't just talk, it listens too. It's hard to talk to people if they aren't even listening to what you have to say. As we said in the last chapter, communication is a two-way street and involves both talking and listening. Since we've already discussed the easy part of this process, let's talk about the hard bit.

Listening is a learned art. There's a technique to it. It doesn't come naturally.

And yet it can be such a ministry if you are capable and willing to sit for hours and listen to someone who needs to be heard.

It is "caring for and being empathetic toward the person who is talking."[1]

There's a world just waiting for someone to listen to it. And this isn't a new phenomenon either. Even in A.D. 65, people wanted to be heard. Seneca, the bright old Roman philosopher, spent his life presenting new and different ideas to his corrupt society. He just wanted people to stop and listen. After Nero ordered him to commit suicide, Seneca exclaimed, in desperation,

> *Listen to me for a day—an hour—*
> *a moment lest I expire in my terrible*
> *wilderness, my lonely silence! O God,*
> *is there no one to listen?*[2]

Although we don't know the exact details about the death of Naomi's husband, it must have been awfully hard for her to be away from her friends and relatives—so alone—at such a time of need. She must have been tempted to feel isolated, too. But unlike the Roman, the Lord supplied her with kind companions, because in verse 8 of chapter 1 Naomi says, "May the Lord show kindness to you, as you have shown to your dead and to me."

When Ruth's and Orpah's husbands died, there must have been an awful lot of listening and caring going on in that household.

But isn't that what the family is for? To be a support system for each other?

Like the time I finished my winter finals at college and excitedly packed my bags because I was going to spend some of the Christmas vacation at Greg's home. We'd planned to drive to Milwaukee after that to be with you. I knew that sometime during the next two weeks, Greg and I were going to become engaged. The big question was when! I'd almost completed my task when the phone rang. It was Dad. He asked if I'd finished my exams and after I responded, "Yes," he proceeded to tell me that Nanna had died. I couldn't believe it. I knew she'd been sick, but hadn't realized exactly how ill. Dad told me that you were in England and would return after the funeral. I asked if he was going over to meet you. He wanted to, he said, but his passport was at the Embassy and they wouldn't give it back. Immediately I suggested that I should fly over. "That would be wonderful, darling," said Dad, and hung up to make the necessary arrangements. He met me at O'Hare Airport to give me my tickets and some much-needed encouragement. "What do I say to Mom?" I asked urgently. I had loved my Nanna so much and was missing her terribly already, but I knew your pain and sorrow must be ten times as acute as mine. "Just sit and listen. That's all you need to do," he replied.

Dad was right. You met me at the airport and we hugged and cried together. Then, during the hour drive to Liverpool, I kept quiet while you explained the events of the past couple of weeks. You needed to talk; to have someone to listen to you. It helped, didn't it?

At that moment when you lent me your listening, loving heart, I realized the interdependence we now enjoyed. Here was my own daughter ministering to me. It was you who suggested we pray together the night before the funeral, you who read me the Scriptures that I could hardly see through my tears, and you who searched for the saving bits of humor in the situation that were the necessary valve for our compressed grief. "She's grown up," I said to myself, "and I need her. She's giving me help and support and I love her for it!"

Somewhere I believed Nanna was smiling. She understood. Hadn't I been able to do the same thing for her the very week before her death? It takes mothers and daughters to really understand. You have to be born to belong to know what that is all about!

You know, Judy, so many people today need a loving, listening ear just as I did. But they use other methods to communicate that fact.

Some ask for help in dramatic ways such as taking drugs, turning to alcohol, or attempting suicide.

What about the kids you worked with in the youth group? Wouldn't they stop by when they were out shopping or on a date? I think they wanted to be heard too!

I enjoyed listening to them. We became good friends because I was willing to take the time to sit patiently and give them my full attention while they talked.

And they were willing to trust you with the information they were sharing.

Isn't that the key—to be trustworthy and nonjudgmental? People aren't going to risk talking with you if they think you'll laugh at them or tell the world. They want to feel secure.

Love endures. If they know you're a leaky listener, they won't unload on you, that's for sure. They need you to be watertight!

When Paul wrote to the believers in Corinth, he told them that love endures. The Greek word has the connotation of "covering." Love covers error and sin. That's why love never gossips. It finds no joy in passing along juicy tidbits of news. Love knows sin hurts God, so why rejoice in it? Love "does not delight in evil but rejoices with the truth" (1 Corinthians 13:6). People have to know it is safe to tell you private things.

Of course, this puts an added burden on the listener. What happens if I receive information in the course of my listening that incriminates another person? How do I handle information that tells me the husband of my best friend is running around, for instance? However you cope with it, a confidence is a confidence and must be treated as such.

Not long ago I received a disturbing letter from a young missionary. She had been under severe stress and had eventually gone to a high-ranking colleague with her troubles. Imagine her dismay to find herself quoted in the mission's monthly magazine the very next issue!

I think Naomi was watertight. Somehow I get the impression Ruth's love story was kept under wraps until it was a fait accompli, don't you?

Yes, I do. And love stories are among the most difficult things to keep under wraps! But, then, love covers because love is concerned with the confidences it receives. It honors the trust placed in it. It never tells tales.

If you're willing to give that opportunity to people, they will beat a path to your door. Unfortunately, there aren't too many people who will take the time and make the effort to do it.

When I went with Dad to visit missionaries in the Third World, I saw the way those isolated people needed a listening ear. It wasn't only rich teaching and encouragement that Dad brought to them, it was the fact that he had time to be a sounding board—a third party who was not in their inner circle.

We enjoyed taking those trips together. I love it when I can go along with Dad and help. I'll never forget being in Africa and visiting a school for missionary children. They were such super kids. Most of them, however, were far away from their parents. I had lots of neat little talks I had prepared for them, but found myself leaving them in my file. They needed my ear, not my mouth!

One beautiful young lady about seventeen years of age was trying to make some pretty important decisions about college. Should she go to the United States or Europe? Could she find a job? What would it all mean to her family? There was no way she could contact her dad and mom as they were translating the Scriptures in the jungle. Reenee was lonely. What a joy it was to lend her my heart and my ears! When I left, she slipped me a little note. It said, "Because you listened to me I learned a lesson. You didn't know me—what I'm really like—but you sympathized and loved me as if you had known me for all of my seventeen years. Thank you for not lecturing, but listening!"

That's wonderful. And what a lesson Reenee has to teach us. We have to learn somehow to listen without lecturing too.

Oh boy, I'm still struggling with that.

When I was young, I didn't want to tell you anything in case I got a lecture!

It's difficult not to come on with a ton of moral platitudes when a child makes a provocative statement.

I remember!

I had to discover that listening doesn't demand a response. We don't always have to say something! I tried to count to fifty before I answered you. Do you recollect when you were just bursting into your teens and you told me all your friends were dating and a certain boy had asked you out? I knew the certain boy was not a Christian and I had met your friends. I panicked. "You can't date," I said, "until you're fifteen." I reckoned that gave me two and a half years' respite. "Well then," you retorted, "when I'm fifteen, I'll choose who I date—Christian or non-Christian— when I date, and how much I date." I opened my mouth to begin lecture number one, entitled "Christians Don't Date Non-Christians." The sermon had three points and a conclusion. For once I heard and heeded that inner voice checking me. "Not now," it said firmly. Somehow I put the lecture back on the shelf of my mind. It was neither the time nor the place for it. I didn't always manage to do that, did I?

No, but by the time I was fifteen, I was a lot more willing to listen! If people know they'll get a lecture every time they come near you, they won't come around very often.

But on the other hand there are times when a lecture is necessary. If a young woman comes to me to tell me that her boyfriend is trying to take advantage of her, I'm not going to send her away without some Christian concept as an alternative.

Of course not. But I think there should be some silence before the lecture begins!

Right! A good listener fights down the impulsive response. He or she needs time to understand the other person and see the full implication of what is being said.

As we are actively listening, we have to be asking ourselves, "What is going on, what's making this person tick, what is on her mind?"

That brings us to comprehension. Hearing is the sensory process by which auditory sounds are received by the ear and transmitted to the listener. Listening is the more complex psychological process involving interpreting and understanding the significance of what's being said.

In other words, what is said is not always what is readily understood! We need to listen for clues. Is this person telling me she feels guilty because she's a lousy homemaker? Or does she really want me to know her marriage is in trouble and they're fighting over the child support for his ex-wife?

When I get tired, I have a short fuse. At such times, Greg will say to me, "We both need to go to bed and get some sleep." Now, I know he doesn't mean "we" at all.

He means you! Just like Dad carving the Sunday joint—sorry, roast—and asking innocently, "Where did you get this meat?" Actually, that can be an absolutely straightforward question. I immediately hear "There's something wrong with it," or, "It must have cost a fortune." I have to be careful not to hear what isn't being said.

I believe that the Christian has a huge advantage at this point. She can learn to listen with the Lord. She can be in prayer—in tune with the God of wisdom who will help her to sort out the complex situations she meets.

Boaz listened with the Lord when Ruth lay down at his feet (Ruth 3:7). He asked himself, "What is she saying? What does this mean?"

Samuel did too. In 1 Samuel 8:21 (NKJV) the Bible tells us, "Samuel heard all the words of the people, and he reported them in the hearing of the Lord." He didn't react to the people's request immediately, but waited until he was given wisdom. He did not offer his own advice, but insisted on seeing it from God's perspective. Then, and only then, he spoke to the people.

That must have been very hard. The people wanted a king like the other nations around them, and Samuel knew this was not God's plan. Yet his response teaches us something. He did not give his own opinion, but waited on the Lord for the answer.

I've learned to say to people, "I need to pray about this, let's get back together again."

A Christian doesn't have to have an opinion about everything, a verse for everybody, or free advice. However, just as there is a time to listen, there is a time to speak—after the listening is over! I can be the finest listener in the world, but I cannot meet the need of the soul. In the end, God has to do that, and so I need to be in touch with Him. One of my favorite passages in the book of Isaiah is:

"The Lord God has given Me
The tongue of the learned,
That I should know how to speak
A word in season to him who is weary.
He awakens Me morning by morning,

He awakens My ear
To hear as the learned. The Lord God has opened My ear;
And I was not rebellious,
Nor did I turn away" (Isaiah 50:4–5, NKJV).

He's the one who will give me the know-how to know what to say. Perhaps I need to concentrate on "the ministry of presence," as someone has so succinctly put it.

Do you think you have to be mature to listen?

Well, if you really aspire to listen, you need to forget yourself, and even your own spiritual life, and turn your attention upward and outward.

I love this little poem you sent me:

I lend a sympathetic ear
to other people's woes
However dull it is to hear their real—
or fancied throes
I pay to every gloomy line
attention undiminished
Because I plan to start on "mine" the
moment they are finished!

I love it too, but it hurts! And yet it's true—our motives for listening are sometimes just that selfish. Self-centered individuals are *not* good listeners.

Sometimes when I've talked to my friends, they haven't looked like they were listening to me. After finishing, I'd ask them if they even heard a word I said. They'd adamantly reply that of course they had caught everything, but I was skeptical. It is so important to look as though you're listening, otherwise people might think you don't care. Many studies have shown that when the talker receives two contradictory messages from the listener, he tends to believe the nonverbal one first.

So I could be preparing dinner in the kitchen and honestly listening to my husband, but he would think I hadn't heard him or didn't care?

Exactly. It's important to make sure our outward appearance says, "I am listening to you!"

I have a terrible time with that. Sometimes on a Sunday morning at church, people will come up and start pouring out their hearts to me. Instead of listening with my eyes, I allow them to wander around the lobby looking for the next person I have to see.

But it isn't just your eyes that are looking past people, your mind isn't concentrating on them either.

I think the two go hand-in-hand. If I'm directly looking at someone, it's a lot easier for me to keep my mind on what she's saying. Dad says that men have an internal switch they can use when their wives are going on and on! But I don't think men are the only ones!

Our whole body language needs to shout, "Come on, let's have it. You're center stage in my thinking right now."

I heard a story about a youth pastor who finally received his own church. He couldn't wait to get back and share with his former boss all that he'd been learning. When he finally had his appointment, he was disillusioned. The whole time he was speaking, the senior pastor was shuffling papers and tidying his desk. After he'd finished, the young pastor said, "Is it too much to ask for five minutes of your time, or are you really too busy to listen?"

Now, to be fair, the pastor might have been listening as well as tidying, but he didn't communicate that. We need to listen without hurry, without the tick of a clock in the back of our minds.

I've heard of some very practical ways to demonstrate that you are listening. For example, if the two parties are facing each other, the one who is listening should lean slightly toward the talker. This says, "Look, I'm giving you all of my attention and turning away from everything else around me."

Once you look as if you're listening, you should say it! For example, ask searching questions. Don't respond to your partner with questions that only need a yes or no answer, because that stops the flow of the conversation.

As when I asked you, "How do you feel about moving to America?" Instead of, "Do you want to move to the United States?"

Yes. That gave me a chance to tell you I didn't want to leave my friends and express some fears about where we would live and what school I'd attend.

Small words and encouraging noises such as "great," "quite so," "uh huh," and "mmm" help too.

If the conversation starts to flag, but you feel that your partner still needs time, you can ask personal questions about her family or personal interests. It's amazing how quickly she'll start up again.

Boaz seemed to have mastered the art of listening. He listened to his servant—"She is the Moabitess who came back from Moab with Naomi" (Ruth 2:6)—and to Ruth—"Why have I found such favor in your eyes, that you should notice me—a foreigner?" (Ruth 2:10). The most difficult task must have been to hear the near kinsman out in front of others when the outcome could have cost him dearly. He didn't interrupt, but let the man have his say. "I cannot redeem it because I might endanger my own estate. You redeem it yourself. I cannot do it"(4:6).

Boaz also encouraged Ruth to listen: "You will listen, my daughter, will you not?" (2:8, NKJV). Although, as we have already said, she was well practiced in the art. Naomi, too, listened. She took time out to pay close attention to Ruth when she came in from work.

I need to follow Naomi's example. Sometimes when Greg arrives home after a long day at the office, I yell "Hi" to him from the kitchen or study and continue on with what I am doing. That isn't right. I should take the time to leave my work and go and ask him about his day. Love listens because love wants to show it cares.

There's a beautiful little picture in Exodus 21 that illustrates exactly what we have been talking about. Slaves that loved their masters and did not want to leave them were told to let the fact be known. The master would then take the slave to a post in the marketplace and pierce his ear with an awl. This would mark the man's ear unmistakably for life. Everyone who saw the mark would know he was a man who had said, "I love my master—I will not go out free" (see Exodus 21:5).

He had pierced ears!

I must admit I think of the story when I put my earrings in! It reminds me that the world that is looking for a listening ear will quickly recognize mine.

It's easy to say, "I love my master," but harder to promise, "I will not go out free."

Of course, it doesn't take much commitment to say, "I love God," but it does to give away my freedom. Listening takes a slavelike attitude to the lordship of Christ. If I am going to have a listening ministry, there will be a cost to myself in time, money, and nervous tension.

Nervous tension! It takes me more nervous energy to sit still and listen than to be physically active!

But the rewards are marvelous. Listening shows me how fortunate I am.

"I cried because I had no shoes until I met a man who had no feet?"

Yes. Giving counsel and encouragement to others has opened up a whole new world to me. I've listened to some appalling things in my time. When someone is telling me their troubles, I keep saying to myself, "Thank you, Lord, for my blessings!" When Dad has had a particularly awful marriage mess on his hands, and puts in endless listening hours, I've noticed he always gives me a big bear hug and says, "Thank you for you, for our marriage, for our love!"

Love listens—using silence to talk
louder than a thousand words—
bending near the sick one
focusing attention
on the need.

Looking as though there's
no one else in the
wide, wide
world
Except the one who needs to talk.

Love is watertight, never leaking
the confidences shared
at midnight—
or at dawn—or in the middle of the day!
Time is irrelevant to love.

Love borrows wisdom from on high
passing on eternity's
information
at the right time and in
the right
way.
Love's ears are open to a shriek
or groan, complaints or
angry shout.
It matters not—love listens.

Talk to Him—you'll see, and you'll be back again,
No one listens like Love!

Talk Time

1. List three ways you can use your body language to show someone you're listening to her.

2. How important is it to be watertight? Can you trust each other with what you share?

3. Can you listen without lecturing? How do you control the impulsive response?

4. Why did these men need a listening ear?

   2 Chronicles 17:15
   Jonah 2:1, 2, 7
   Lamentations 3:52–57
   Jeremiah 38:6–7

Love Triumphs

CHAPTER TEN

Love never fails—that's what God says. In the end, love wins out. See it demonstrated here in grand fashion:

So Boaz took Ruth and she became his wife. Then he went to her, and the Lord enabled her to conceive, and she gave birth to a son. The woman said to Naomi: 'Praise be to the Lord, who this day has not left you without a kinsman-redeemer. May he become famous throughout Israel! He will renew your life and sustain you in your old age. For your daughter-in-law, who loves you and who is better to you than seven sons, has given him birth." Then Naomi took the child, laid him in her lap and cared for him (Ruth 4:13–16).

The names of the characters in this story fascinate me. We could have a great time spiritualizing them. Elimelech means "my God is king." He married Naomi, which means "pleasure." When "my God is king" commits himself to "pleasure" it should come as no surprise to find the children named "sickness" and "pining"! Boaz means "strength" and Ruth, "friendship." When they wed, the result was Obed, "worship."

It is enough to say that Boaz and Ruth had been given first place in the purposes of God. Jehovah had been given first place in their affections. Christ Himself would be found in their lineage: "Also the neighbor women gave him a name, saying, 'Naomi has a son.' And they named him Obed. He was the father of Jesse, the father of David" (Ruth 4:17).

When Christ is given His rightful place in our family, then God gets the glory. I don't mean a family makes it because they all attend church together. Many families are falling apart this week who shared a hymnbook last week! Relationships will be truly strong only if Christ is Lord of the individual heart and, therefore, head of the corporate whole.

Some time ago, I was listening to one of Billy Graham's daughters talking about her wonderful family. She mentioned the many generations before them that had loved and served the Lord. I felt a certain envy. Then she said, "It wasn't always so. There was a time when, as far as we know, one side of our family were unbelievers. At some point, they came to Christ and started a godly heritage. We shouldn't spend our time wishing we'd had a godly grandma. We can begin now by making sure of our own commitment."

When Dad and I got married, we took as a life text, "As for me and my house, we will serve the Lord" (Joshua 24:15). This does not mean "as for my husband," it means "as for all of us." We will serve the Lord; we will do it together. Mother and children will not be standing on the sidelines applauding Daddy as he runs the race that is set before him, but we will all be pounding the track beside him, reaching for the prize together!

The problem we had was the spectators. We couldn't help but hear all the things they shouted as they watched us. Even back in those days people told us you wouldn't make it spiritually because Dad was gone so much of the time.

That must have been hard for you because you knew he was involved in God's calling.

It was terribly difficult. I prayed fervently for you children because I wanted you to turn out all right.

But you didn't just pray; you made sure that we were involved in the ministry too. You've often asked me how I felt about Dad's being gone. To tell you the truth, it didn't bother me too much because that was the way it had always been. I didn't know anything different. From my earliest years, we had helped in Dad's ministry.

Remember the warehouse? Sometimes I still can't believe you bought that huge, run-down building.

Well, it was bigger than the little cow barn we'd been using, and we needed space.

It was also perfect for kids.

When we first found it, I couldn't believe the potential; old oak beams, crooked chimneys, and all sorts of other rustic possibilities. It was a perfect place for a youth center, but we couldn't afford it.

Didn't someone suggest that you start a nursery school and use the money from that to pay for the building?

Yes, that was the only way we could have taken it on.

We were very young then, so you took us to school with you. Even at the age of three, I was involved in your ministry. For me this meant play-ing with sand, water, and clay; painting pictures and singing nursery rhymes. Now I know I was caught up in the purposes of God.

The first time I went visiting in the area around our house, I took you kids with me. I knew God wanted me to stop dreaming about the future and the time when Dad and I could minister together. I needed to reach out in my own back yard. My neighbors were little old ladies who had to hear about Jesus too. But I had a baby and two toddlers. What would I do with them? "Take them with you," whispered a small voice inside.

"Don't forget, 'as for me and my house, we will serve the Lord.' " You seemed terribly small to be beginning your Christian careers, but I put Pete in his pram and took you and Dave by the hand and off we went. I'll always remember knocking at the rose-bedecked cottage of a near neighbor and asking her to come to a home Bible study I had started. A look of horror spread over her face. I didn't think it sounded that bad. Then David stepped forward with a flourish and presented the little old lady with a beautiful bunch of red tulips. Deciding to throw himself in the spirit of the thing and involve himself in the purposes of God, he had carefully cleaned out her front yard! Then there was Grotty Bob.

Grotty Bob? Who was he?

When Dad was home, he instigated a street ministry in Manchester. Together with a friend, they obtained the use of the basement of a condemned building. They turned it into a Christian coffee bar called "The Catacombs." All sorts and conditions of men or, rather, teens found their way there. One, who happened to be a drug pusher, was called Grotty Bob. One night, Dad brought him home to stay for a while! A few mornings later, I walked into the living room and found Dave perched on his knee, stroking his long, greasy locks. I was just in time to hear Dave say, "You look like Jesus!" Grotty Bob melted! "That's the nicest thing anyone ever said to me," he spluttered in a choked voice. "I bet it is," I muttered grimly, rescuing my child. But you know, Dave didn't need rescuing. Grotty Bob did! I was reminded of that at bedtime when my four-year-old prayed for him. God had prepared a work for our family, and we as parents had to remember that.

Although Dave's action wasn't exactly what you had in mind, he was learning that serving God doesn't have to be boring. Dave told me that he loved having wild teenagers in our home, and I enjoyed picking flowers, taking long walks, and playing with my friends in the sandbox at nursery school. You were helping us to see that serving Jesus together included fun times too.

Capernwray also provided a lot of special times for you kids.

I guess there aren't too many children who grow up near a huge castle. We had such fun playing hide and seek and sliding down the huge banisters.

What about helping to shear the sheep and riding on top of the bales of hay? That was a marvelous playground for you children. But it was more than that. Every week you'd meet a vibrant group of young people from all over the world who were coming to the Bible school to better equip themselves to serve God. Those teenagers spoiled you three. They spent endless hours paying attention to you. All of that had to influence you in some way.

I'm sure it did, but we had other models, too. There was the staff. There was Chris, who became a loving and caring big brother to Dave. Dave became his shadow, and Chris took him everywhere—feeding the cattle and chopping the trees down in the park. There was construction going on all the time. I guess that was because we were part of a missionary center, which meant a do-it-yourself philosophy, and Dave pushed barrels of dirt, climbed scaffolding, and laid brick with the "big boys" all through one summer holiday. I'll never forget his face when he was paid just as much as the other boys who were twice his size!

He learned that God's work took sweat and effort. He saw a desire for excellence in the workmanship those young men put forth. Where else could those sort of invaluable lessons be learned?

Seeing people make hundreds of beds every Saturday and cooking gigantic quantities of food, not because they particularly enjoyed it, but because that was the best way they could serve God, taught me many things.

What?

Well, they showed me that everyone wasn't called by God to travel the world speaking about Jesus. Some people had to do the practical things, the obvious tasks. I could be part of that! Just because I wasn't ministering in America didn't mean I couldn't be involved. I was helping hundreds of people to meet Jesus by being willing to let my dad go!

Capernwray was good to me, too. Like Ruth, I found myself in the midst of a community of caring people, and like the women of Bethlehem, there was a common joy at the birth of my babies. The bells in the clock tower rang out the night you were born, Judy. The whole village knew you had arrived! So even though Dad had the lonely part, both of us were encouraged to see that God looks after the people who are precious to us if we look after the people who are precious to Him!

When we came to America, I discovered that God's world wasn't only full of teenagers, but it also included people of all ages.

After thirteen years with the youth ministry, it was a real change of gears for all of us, wasn't it?

Yes, it was a higher gear—a more hectic pace!

Part of that was because of our philosophy of always having an open house. Now even more people traipsed through our home.

Do you remember the wedding we had in our living room on Christmas day?

How could I ever forget? Dad had no alternative because one set of parents refused to step inside a church! But it was different.

I was trying to help you get Christmas dinner ready. Unfortunately, there weren't any doors between the kitchen and the living room. Every time I'd clang two pots together, you'd hurriedly whisper, "Be quiet!"

Then there was the media ministry we ran from our basement.

Groups of women would come to put together hundreds of tapes to send out all over the world—

While upstairs your friends would be swarming all over the house—

And you would be trying to cook dinner—

And write books—

While Dad tried to find a corner of the house to have a church meeting.

Then our fellowship began to grow at such a rate that we decided to have an open house every few weeks to keep in touch with everyone. All those whose last names began with "A" through "F" came first.

We had about eighty people at a time.

More, I believe.

That was when we had already outgrown the church building and were meeting in a theater. So Sunday school had to be held in homes.

Guess whose?

Those days were fun. I must have absorbed the idea of not only giving my heart to God, but also my home. When Greg and I were newly married and working with the youth group, God showed me very quickly that our apartment didn't belong to us. We were only borrowing it from Him. It was really His to do with as He pleased, when He pleased.

I think that's one of the hardest lessons. You have to give your "whens" to God if you're going to serve Him wholeheartedly.

Sometimes God chose late hours to bring a confused teenager to our apartment. That was not the time I would have ideally picked, but it was all in God's perfect timing.

That reminds me of the story of Martha and Mary. I turned to that little passage in Luke 10 over and over again. Jesus loved to catch His breath in that home. Every time He had finished a tour of ministry or needed some rest or refreshment, He would visit those friends. This time Martha was doing all the practical things while Mary sat at Jesus' feet and listened to His word. Martha became frustrated, telling the Lord to command her sister to help her Jesus gently rebuked her, reminding her that Mary had chosen "the better part."

I had to remember to keep close to the Lord or, like Martha, I became irritated with the Lord, my sisters, and the world in general! The Bible says Martha was "cumbered" (KJV) by much service. The word means "distracted." I don't think you ever master the lesson she learned once and for all. Being a Mary is hard for me. I love to be busy, to be running here and there, excited and creative, but if the whole thing isn't motivated by Jesus, then, like Martha, I'll hear His rebuke at the end of the day.

As we've said, giving Christ your heart means giving Him your home. Martha and Mary showed you that, you demonstrated it to me, and now I hope to be a model for the next generation!

The old generation is benefiting too. Dad and I are already enjoying the fruits of relinquishment.

Naomi gave Boaz to Ruth, Boaz gave Ruth a child, and Ruth gave little Obed into Naomi's arms. The fruits of relinquishment came back to them, too! It is in giving that we receive. We die to live, we give to receive. That is what true Christianity is all about. Love overcomes all obstacles—God's sort of love.

Look what happened to Ruth and Naomi's relationship after Ruth and Boaz married. Ruth is described by the women of the city as "your daughter-in-law, who loves you, … is better to you than seven sons," (Ruth 4:15), so it doesn't sound as if their love diminished or their relationship faltered. I believe that's what should happen after marriage. It's such a shame that there are so many in-law problems.

Perhaps there are so many because the marriage relationship doesn't have the central place in everyone's thinking.

Also because sons and daughters are still emotionally or materially dependent on their parents.

Right before Greg and I married, when you and I were having one of our mother-daughter talks, you told me that once I was married, I couldn't come running home to you. I felt a little hurt and surprised. It took me time to understand that you were really saying, "Jude, you aren't going to be dependent on me anymore. That doesn't mean we can't enjoy a beautiful relationship, but it will be something new and different from what we've experienced for the last twenty-one years." I was glad you told me that because so many parents don't help their children leave and cleave.

It was imperative you understood what leaving and cleaving was all about. Leaving means to leave the old lifestyle. I know of marriages where the husband insists on continuing to go hunting, fishing, and camping "with the boys" after the wedding day, without even missing a step! Or the wife refuses to stop letting her mother make her decisions. The arguments are bound to begin. As the honeymoon tiptoes out the door, the divorce peers around the corner! Men and women have to leave the old way of life. Things have to change. Cleaving involves sticking it out together when things get sticky.

I've learned what it really means to shift my emotional and material dependency from you to Greg. When we were first married, I almost auto-

matically reached for the telephone whenever I had a certain problem or very good news to share. Usually before I finished dialing your number, I realized what I was doing, and I made sure Greg knew about it first before calling you. It takes time to readjust emotionally and materially too.

When we were first married and Greg was at grad school, I found a job that paid OK, but it still didn't seem as if there'd ever be enough money to take care of all the bills. I learned that I needed to depend on God and Greg for everything to work out all right. We decided to have a little blue book to write down every penny we spent. Even if I bought a pack of gum, I recorded my purchase. Our income was also written down. Then, at the end of the month, I'd add up how much we earned and spent, praying that the former would be greater than the latter. It usually was; God was so good to us. He taught me that He would always be there for Greg and me if we lived within our means.

It's amazing the things we can quite happily do without when we have to.

Our culture is so different from that of biblical times. It's hard to draw modern parallels when those people lived so close together all their lives instead of moving miles away from each other as we have done. Because they lived together in the community, they could help each other by sharing their land and their animals. The older women became thoroughly involved in the grandchildren's upbringing, too.

I like that idea! I'm sad that Nanna was so far away in England when we were growing up.

I think grandparents have an immense contribution to make to a family. It's terribly sad to see the way so many elderly people while away their sunset years in virtual isolation. And yet if parents were given a "proper" place within the family, it might be different.

It's up to the young couple to take the initiative and decide what place *that should be. It was Ruth who placed the baby into her mother-in-law's arms. Naomi didn't wrestle the child away from her!*

In our society, families seem to get smaller, but in Ruth's day, the circle widened.

Ours has expanded too; it's just that we're so scattered.

But that doesn't mean we can't share each other's joys and discoveries! I think it's special that you have good relationships with your sisters-in-law. You aren't just relatives, you're really good friends.

I've been working at those new relationships, too, telling myself many times, "Judy is married, and Greg is taking care of her now." I've tried to get to know him as thoroughly as possible and have even taken "his side" in conversations or debates when my natural inclination has been to leap to your defense.

I've noticed that! I sort of like it—I think.

It's just my way of sending a message to Greg. I'm saying, "I know you and Judy are a couple now—and I want you to know I know." As long as my relationship grows with Greg, our new relationship will develop.

Do you remember the time Greg and I had a newly-married tiff and I called you in tears? The first thing you said to me was, "Judy, does Greg know you are calling me?" "He told me to," I replied!

That made me smile. He knew he had an ally. This is not to say all my mother-hackles don't go up when my "baby" is under the gun, but I know the best thing I can do is to let Greg understand that Dad and I are for you as a couple! That means forgetting to be partisan. Dad and I often say, "Aren't our kids good to us?" We are amazed you all want our company and enjoy us as friends. We love it!

I think Naomi enjoyed her happy experience, too. I suspect Boaz became very fond of Naomi. Obed was his baby, but he had no objection to the older woman taking up residence in his child's life. That family made it to interdependence.

And so have we—we are our own people and yet we care more deeply for each other than ever before. Dave and Pete are pastors and we have a ministry together.

And yet the choice goes on. Daily, the decision to love has to be made, and each of us is responsible before God to make it. To love or not to love, Judy, that is the eternal question!

The Choice
To Love or Not to Love

"That's that," said Love, looking at His empty cross.

"Is it final?" asked the loved one.

"Yes very," replied Love.

"What happens when the wind blows?"

"Easy—we hang onto each another."

"What happens if we let go?"

"Love never lets go!"

"What if I want out?"

"There's no escape," answered Love soberly.

"That makes me feel sort of—trapped. I don't know if I can breathe—
I get claustrophobia when I'm confined to a small space."

"I don't know what 'small' is," replied Love riding on the wings of the wind.

"There's a great freedom in consistency," he continued—returning breathless
with joy,

"But you'll have to find that out for yourself."

"I don't know if I'm ready to be loved like that—"

"That's your privilege."

"I think I'll wait a bit if you don't mind—
Will you be here when I come back?"

"Yes."

"I don't know if I like being that sure about you—
it sort of loses the challenge, if you know what I mean.
The challenge of 'making you love me'"

"But if you 'made me' love you, you could 'make me' stop.
That's an awful lot of power to handle!"

"Aren't you glad you can't?" "I guess so."

"Go away," said Love (love always lets go).

"Find out what you want from life.
Only be gentle with the ones that you love 'your way.'
Selfish love diminishes people—
When you can't love anymore and there's still an awful
lot of loving to be done …

Call—and I will come—
You'll need me then!"

Notes

Chapter One: Love Is a Choice

1. *Significa (April 8, 1984). Idea submitted by Harold Hielter, Silver Spring, Md.*
2. Helen Keller, *The Story of My Life (New York: Doubleday, 1904),* p. 21.

Chapter Two: Love Is a Commitment

1. *Ruth A. Tucker,* From Jerusalem to Irian Jaya *(Michigan: Academic Books, 1983), p. 264.*

Chapter Three: Love Is Forgiveness

1. *Corrie ten Boom,* The Hiding Place *(Lincoln, Va.: Chosen Books, 1971) p. 215.*

Chapter Five: Love Remains

1. *"dependence," (3),* The American Heritage Dictionary, *Second Edition (Boston: Houghton Mifflin, 1982), p. 382.*
2. *C. S. Lewis,* The Four Loves *(New York: Harcourt, Brace and Co., 1960).*
3. *Lewis, p. 13.*
4. *Lewis, pp. 12–13.*
5. *Erich Fromm,* The Oxford Book of Aphorisms *(New York: Oxford University Press, 1983).*

Chapter Six: Love Lets Go

1. *People (25 June 1984).*

Chapter Seven: Love Is a Teacher

1. *Richard L. Strauss,* Confident Children and How They Grow *(Wheaton: Tyndale, 1975).*

Chapter Eight: Love Talks

1. H. *Norman Wright*, Communication: Key to Your Marriage (*Ventura, Calif.: Regal Books, rev. 2000*).
2. Webster's New World Dictionary of the American Language (*Cleveland, Ohio: William Collins Publishers, Inc., 1979*).
3. *ibid.*

Chapter Nine: Love Listens

1. H. *Norman Wright*, Communication: Key to Your Marriage (*Ventura, Calif.: Regal Books, rev. 2000*).
2. *Freely quoted from sermon.*